MICHAEL L. GECZI was born in Cleveland, Ohio and attended Western New England College. From 1970 to 1977, he was an editor and reporter for *The Wall Street Journal*, covering the stock, bond, and futures markets. Subsequently, he was Supervising Editor for business news for the Associated Press. Currently, the author is Markets and Investments Editor for *Business Week* magazine. His articles have appeared in many publications, including *The New York Times* and *The New York Daily News*.

FUTURES: THE ANTI-INFLATION INVESTMENT

MICHAEL L. GECZI

With Introductions by
Neil J. Aslin, Senior Vice-President,
Conticommodity Services, Inc.
and
Jean M. Blin, Senior Vice-President,
New York Futures Exchange

 A DISCUS BOOK/PUBLISHED BY AVON BOOKS

FUTURES: THE ANTI-INFLATION INVESTMENT is
an original publication of Avon Books. This work has
never before appeared in book form.

AVON BOOKS
A division of
The Hearst Corporation
959 Eighth Avenue
New York, New York 10019

Copyright © 1980 by Michael L. Geczi
Published by arrangement with the author
Library of Congress Catalog Card Number: 80-66730
ISBN: 0-380-75713-3

First Discus Printing, August, 1980

DISCUS TRADEMARK REG. U.S. PAT. OFF. AND IN
OTHER COUNTRIES, MARCA REGISTRADA, HECHO EN
U.S.A.

Printed in the U.S.A.

For LJG, who is my present;
GJG and LMG, who are my past;
And KDG and AMG, who are my future.

Contents

Acknowledgments

In writing a book, nothing comes easy. Time, effort, and research obviously are factors that weigh heavily in the successful completion of any manuscript. But those obstacles, when successfully vaulted, do not insure that a manuscript—especially one dealing with as complex a subject as commodity futures—is structured in such a way that it will be easily understood by readers. Compounding the problem also is the fact that this book is aimed at the novice futures investor, so I have attempted to build this work with those thoughts in mind.

This book is highly departmentalized (my thinking is that two hundred consecutive pages of gray prose would not be read) so that answers to questions can be looked up quickly. Moreover, when complex subjects are dealt with, I have attempted to keep the explanations in conversational form so that the reader would not think that he or she was reading a college textbook.

I am not a commodity trader myself; I am a journalist. I wanted this book to be professional in its writing and in the information it provides. To accomplish this end, therefore, I needed the help of many kind people—who are professionals in the market—to make it all come together.

The list is endless, but let me cite just a few: my employers at McGraw-Hill Inc. and *Business Week*, for allowing me to do such a project; Rich Edelman at Daniel J. Edelman of New York Inc.; Neil Aslin, Jack Zaner, Phil Tiger and all the other great people at ContiCommodity Services Inc.; Ed Lee at the Chicago Board of Trade; Don Sarno at Clayton Brokerage Co. of St. Louis; the folks who are building the New York Futures Exchange, and Laura Pavlicek, whose typing magic is beyond description.

MICHAEL L. GECZI

Introduction

For those of us involved with the commodity futures industry, July 23, 1979, was a date of great significance.

It was on that day that the United States Department of Labor put its stamp of legitimacy on our business by ruling that "a prudent man" could now consider futures speculation to be a viable investment. Now, for the first time, even a pension-fund manager could participate in the futures market, a booming business which has been growing at nearly a 40-percent rate for each of the past two years.

The commodity futures industry has benefited from the evolution of an investment attitude that first manifested itself in the "go-go" securities funds of the middle 1960s. Though these funds often failed, wrecked by the 1969 "bear" market, they did make significant contributions to investment history. They showed that investors wanted to shift emphasis to performance and away from the buy-and-hold tradition endorsed for decades by owners of blue-chip stocks and bonds. It was the vehicle of go-go funds that was wrong—not the attitude of the investor.

The modern investor seeks attractive situations which he moves into and out of in a relatively short time period.

With this buy-and-sell approach, the risk of error increases, but so does the potential for profit. Many have been willing to make that exchange.

The preeminent concern with performance has only been heightened by frequent reminders that money is buying less today than yesterday. Investors have concluded that inflation is not a temporary phenomenon. There is greater regard than ever for assets perceived as having lasting value. They are seen as the only respite from a loss of purchasing power that has continued unabated for the past forty years.

Interest in futures trading among individuals began to be piqued in the early 1970s as worldwide events thrust these markets to the fore. The major grain shipments to the Soviet Union in 1972 pushed prices higher and made export sales a domestic issue. The sudden disappearance of the anchovy from the shores of Peru in 1973, for example, eliminated a traditional source of animal feed and caused soybean prices to quadruple. In 1974–1975, sugar prices moved ahead from 10 cents to 65 cents a pound, as an unexpected production shortfall caught the industry with low inventories. Finally, Americans were allowed to own gold in 1975 for the first time in thirty-two years, making gold again the world market commodity in which price is determined by fundamental factors, not pegged artificially by the United States government.

In this investment environment, one in which participants seek more short-run opportunities, commodities have great appeal because prices are determined by real supply-and-demand factors that change every day. There are no takeover attempts nor stock splits which can affect value, only variables such as the weather or inflation. The data necessary for making decisions in futures is available in an almost constant stream on wire services, unlike the comparatively arbitrary quarterly earnings or size of dividend which hinge on the decisions of a company's management or board of directors.

The futures exchanges have done much to interest a wider group of investors in their products by offering an ever more diverse set of futures contracts. Beginning from generally agricultural backgrounds, the exchanges have expanded to encompass financial instruments, currencies, heating oil, and metals. With more items to trade, it is more true than ever that there is *always* an opportunity in one of the futures markets for an investor. Exchanges also are no longer timid about competing with one another, as many offer the same contracts, adding more liquidity to the markets.

Just as the futures exchanges are putting forth new contracts on a regular basis, the futures brokerage houses are developing new vehicles for participating in the markets. For the investor who does not have the time or inclination to follow the markets on a continuing basis, firms now offer both managed accounts and mutual funds, in which the onus is on the professional money manager to take advantage of opportunities that present themselves.

All of which brings us to Mr. Geczi's book.

Our research at ContiCommodity into the thinking and preferences of investors clearly reveals great interest in futures trading by persons who have yet to make their first trade. The research shows also a major reluctance to trade on the part of a large group of otherwise qualified futures traders based on their lack of understanding of futures. It is not so much the futures they fear as it is their unfamiliarity with what is improperly perceived to be a highly complex subject.

Presumably, if more was done to educate investors, the reluctance this group admits would give way to a willingness to try the leverage offered by futures contracts and the volatility of prices which offers the opportunity for gain. This book is organized to present a complete look at the specimen: the market's vernacular, what's involved in opening an account, how contracts are traded, the products and exchanges, and, finally, personal trading methods.

From my own observation, its most valuable message is this: In the futures market you are dealing with eventual reality, and no one knows in advance what that reality will be. Your estimate can be as good as the next person's if you work at it, for price discovery in the futures market is basically an exciting exercise in deductive reasoning.

NEIL J. ASLIN
Executive Vice President
ContiCommodity Services Inc.

Risks are routinely—if not blindly—borne every day by each of us. Habits, emotional complacency, and intellectual inertia all combine to make risk-bearing less worrisome than a sober analysis would suggest. Yet, experience, personal liability statutes, and sheer fear have also created a demand for some risk-sharing arrangements—insurance contracts. These contracts, however, appear as an economic necessity, not as a matter of choice. The risk of personal ruin is the chief motivation; far from any hope of large monetary gain.

It is thus paradoxical to suggest that the same economic reality, risk, could be dealt with constructively by individuals, not as something to guard against but as something to profit from. The realization of this fact is probably the first lesson to be learned from Mike Geczi's book. Here we are not talking about purchasing shares in insurance companies. Rather, we are referring to participation in commodity futures markets. These markets have existed for over a hundred years in the United States and have, occasionally, flourished in other cultures and other times. But the advent of effective telecommunications and the growth of market information networks make our time particularly opportune for individual participation in the markets. The principle is simple enough to state: contracts for futures delivery of specific amounts of given grades of deliverable commodities are traded on an organized exchange. The "short" agrees to sell to the "long" at a price agreed upon today. Delivery is delayed while price is "locked in." Clearly, if I need copper in known quantities six months hence, it is far preferable to know its price today rather than remain exposed to the vagaries of fluctuating copper prices over the next six months. Who will assume such awesome obligation—namely, to deliver an agreed upon amount "forward" at a price fixed today? Copper producers may well wish to lock in future revenues. But, since I can always buy back the futures contract I sold before the delivery month—at whatever new market price which now prevails—I may feel comfortable trusting my superior foresight and price-forecasting talent to enter such a contract without any intention of actually taking or effecting delivery of the underlying actual commodity. If I choose to speculate on a future price drop and I "short" (sell) the futures contract, my gain will materialize if subsequent price drops do occur and allow me to go "long" (buy) in the same contract, and net out a profit from the double transaction. The alternative, of course, is that I am wrong and prices do not drop, but rise, yielding a loss to me and a gain to the other party in the contract. Efficient markets notwithstanding, human faith in the accuracy of its forecasts have made commodity futures speculating common. And, indeed, everyone can usually cite some impressive example of extraordinary wealth amassed by such dealings.

The obvious question then is: should one consider trading commodities, and if so, how does one go about it? Many other issues need attention: which commodities should one choose? Agricultural, metals, or the fast-growing financial futures—namely, currencies and interest-bearing debt instruments such as three-month U.S. Treasury bills or four-year T-notes? Where should I trade if competing exchanges offer similar type contracts? How can I arbitrage between exchanges? Between contract months? Between different types of contracts? How do I pick a broker? What is a futures commission merchant (FCM)? What are the risks of commodity trading? And, the returns? An overall, clear, comprehensive and down-to-earth account of futures trading is required. To date, much has been written for the specialist in the field. But not everyone aspires to become an expert on the economics of futures trading. Nor does he need to if he simply wishes to add commodities to his portfolio. What he needs is a convenient reference book covering the fundamentals and dealing with the unavoidable questions of "how to."

Mike Geczi's book provides such an account of futures trading. It is clear and well written; it deals effectively with basic material in an easy style. It should help to demystify what has all too often been thought of as an unnecessarily arcane subject best left to professionals. An informed public is the key to efficient use of these markets and to smoother, broader participation by investors. As the futures industry grows with the development of numerous new products—for example, financial futures—and the entry of well-established major exchanges into the futures field, the need for an accessible yet comprehensive account of futures has become all the more important. Mike's book goes a long way toward meeting this need. It should become a standard addition to the basic reference library of the individual investor and help him make his transition into futures smoother.

JEAN M. BLIN
Senior Vice President
New York Futures Exchange

I. The Futures Market: Its Participants, Both Colorful and Dull

Commodity futures.

To most people, these two words are an immediate turnoff. Even those of us who have dabbled in stocks and bonds and who have some idea of what the futures markets are all about are intimidated by the words.

Commodity futures.

Yet despite the intricate components that make commodity futures the most exciting investing medium in the world, such as technical and fundamental analysis, day trading and long-term trading, and even the mundane pork belly, the futures markets are also the most down-to-earth financial arena in the world. And it is not because of the bacon we fry each morning or the ever-growing value we place on gold. It is because of the people that make up the market.

Indeed, no financial marketplace would be a viable entity without the wide assortment of characters that constitute its heartbeat. Young or old, aggressive or conservative, wealthy or not so wealthy, it is the participants in a financial marketplace who provide its liquidity and volatility and who make it an arena in which a small nest egg can either be parlayed into a fortune or whittled away into nothing.

And the commodity futures markets are no exception. In fact, the cast of characters starring in "The Commodity Futures Markets" may have among its ranks the most colorful people in any securities market. How they respond to market and world events, and accumulate and liquidate positions in response to those events, often can be more educational for the novice commodity futures trader than any professional course offered. With that in mind, let's take a close look at several personalities who make up the world of commodity futures.

The Arbitrageur
("All That Glitters Is Not Gold")

To look at Mark sitting behind his huge desk in his beautifully paneled office, a visitor would not think that this man was any different from any other pin-striped, buttoned-down securities industry official. Pictures of his beautiful wife and equally beautiful children adorn both his huge desk and the glittering walls, as do pictures of his sailboat and his lake-front house.

Obviously, this guy has it made. There's money in his pocket. There's money in his bank. There's money in the securities he owns, and one can only imagine what his regular house looks like considering the size of the beach house in the pictures. Not only that, but he still looks young, thirty-seven or so. And he probably has been in this line of work for so long that it now comes so easily to him that working is almost like stealing money.

Wrong.

Mark is highly successful; that much is true. And he does have a significant income, both from what he is paid by the large commodities house that employs him as well as from his outside investments. But there is nothing easy about the line of work that Mark is in, and the huge pot of coffee and the overflowing ashtray on his desk are the first clues.

In point of fact, Mark is a ragged bundle of nerves who uses the stimulation of cigarettes and coffee to keep both his mind and body alert and keen during the course of a workday. And that workday often can be sixteen or eighteen hours long, for Mark is an arbitrageur, a futures market specialist who simultaneously buys and sells contracts in two different commodities—or the same commodity in two different marketplaces—in the expectation that the discrepancy in prices between the two sides will result in profits.

"Arbitrageurs are supposed to be shoot-from-the-hip guys with absolutely no nerves," he says, while drawing on his cigarette and scanning the cathode-ray terminal on his desk which displays up-to-the-minute prices in markets throughout the world. "But it isn't always the nerveless sorts who end up in arbitrage. If that was the case, there would be a hell of a lot more stevedores coming in from the docks to make arbitrage plays. The fact of the matter is that some of us have a talent for finding the price discrepancies, and that is why we are arbitrageurs."

Indeed, while trading commodities futures is primarily a high-risk business (some estimates say that at least 92 percent of all traders lose money) no sector of the market, at least on the surface, possesses the risks and the degree of difficulty that does arbitrage. Because the arbitrageur is trying to profit from just very small discrepancies in prices between two markets, the margin for error, both in timing and in executing a transaction, is very small. Therefore, decisive actions are the key to this type of trading.

Despite Mark's success as an arbitrageur over the years, he is the first one to point out that to be a success in the futures market a person should not attempt to be a generalist with fairly good knowledge about all commodities. Instead, he insists, the trader should determine which types of contracts—grains, foodstuffs, financial futures—he can deal best with and then concentrate solely on those instruments.

"For me, the arbitrage possibilities exist in the foreign currency markets," he confesses. "So that is where I have developed my expertise and that is where I concentrate all my efforts. There are profits to be made in currency arbitrage and I would be foolish to waste my time gambling in an area that I knew less about."

Besides that expertise, Mark stresses that there are four key requirements that make an arbitrageur a success:

• "When you are trading the same commodity in two different markets it is of the utmost importance that your market presence is extremely large. If you don't take huge positions, the commissions you have to pay to assume those positions will just eat up any of the profits that you are able to build up." As a rule, he says, the positions he assumes in the foreign currency markets are well into the hundreds-of-thousands-of-dollars area, so that even the slightest discrepancy in price when multiplied times the number of contracts held will produce a hefty enough profit so that Mark can quickly get out of the position.

• "You can't be an arbitrageur in Chicago and play New York markets versus Chicago markets without knowing the New York situation as well as you do the one in your own town," he says as he enters a transaction that puts him long West German marks on the Chicago Mercantile Exchange and short marks on the New York Mercantile Exchange. "I can't wait for the screen on my desk to print out numbers to show me what is going on in a different market to make a decision. By that time, it probably will be too late to capitalize on it." What he has done over the years, therefore, is to carefully build up a network of specialists in markets around the world who will alert him to always-changing supply, demand, and price considerations that allow him to act decisively at just the right time. In return, Mark reciprocates the favors by giving those "sources" advice on how to invest their funds.

• "An arbitrageur must have a good 'backroom' working for him because the volume and frequency of his trades are what produces profits, and if his 'tickets' aren't processed quickly, that small profit per ticket that he aims for will disappear," he says. In fact, says Mark, those arbitrageurs who do not work for large commission houses with their own internal processing capability often spend more time in setting up their operations, in looking for the "perfect" processing operation with which to work.

• "And last but not least, an arbitrageur must be both knowledgeable and decisive," he says as he gets off the phone to inform his visitor that the West German mark positions he had assumed earlier that day had already produced a one-day profit of 10 percent, or an annual return of nearly 3,700 percent.

Mark's trading strategies appear simple: going long in a market when prices are low and short when they are high.

That logic is simple and most investors realize how to structure those positions. But Mark, an arbitrageur, really never assumes a position, for he always is simultaneously long in one market, or one commodity, and short in another. For him, a transaction always has two legs.

"A lot of people look down on arbitrageurs and sort of paint us as these buzzardlike creatures with a lot a money and muscle who just squeeze profits out of a market because of our sheer strength and large positions," he says. "But we also provide a lot of benefit to the futures markets. We provide liquidity, we inject funds to keep the market going. We are always there to take one side of a transaction.

"We may make a lot of money," he says, lighting another cigarette, "but we also help others to make a lot too."

The Cross-Hedger
("Better Safe Than Sorry")

Dressed in blue jeans and a work shirt, and with a suntan that surely would be the envy of most participants in the commodity futures arena, Jason is just one of the growing legion of cattle ranchers who are coming to use the hedging properties of futures investments more and more to counteract the damaging effects that runaway inflation is having on feed costs. "For the cattleman, the cost of feeding his herd is the most vital ingredient in running a profitable enterprise," he says. "And those costs are running up so quickly that we are just getting killed."

In fact, Jason has increased his profit per animal by 10 percent by employing hedging tactics.

Walking across the vast green lawn that separates his main house from one of the auxiliary buildings, he smiles as he recounts the event that made him see the light. "Increased foreign demand for grain was causing grain prices to jump all over the lot. Grain is our primary feed and I didn't really have a handle on what our future grain costs would be, so I really couldn't determine what kind of prices I needed to get from my heifers to make up for the feed costs," he says.

But he had a buyer and he had to make a decision.

"It was February, and the guy who ran the feedlot operation upstate decided he wanted delivery of 314 heifers in
September," he says. Recounting the event now, he says
that he took a gulp and agreed to the delivery. How much
profit did he feel he wanted to make from the sale? "The
futures price of corn at that time was $2.25¼ per bushel,
so we set that as our target profit."

To hedge the transaction, Jason bought two contracts of
December corn futures at a price of $2.25¼ per contract.
The contracts, comprising 10,000 bushels of corn, approx-
imated the amount of corn he felt he needed that fall.

Entering his house and walking into the spacious and
well-decorated den, Jason freely admits that he is not an
expert at trading commodity futures. Sitting down in an
easy chair near the fireplace, he continues: "No, I'm a
rancher, I'm not a commodities trader. But I am beginning
to understand the key to hedging: the difference between
cash prices and futures prices. And if understanding that
difference can help me to be a more successful rancher
then I am all for it."

In structuring the hedge on that first transaction, Jason
studied the difference—known as the basis—between spot
prices and futures prices. He had anticipated that corn
prices would rise, but was not sure when that uptrend
would materialize. So, therefore, he decided to take a long
position when the basis appeared to be the smallest. In
February, when he bought the corn contracts for $2.25¼,
corn was selling in the cash market for $2.23¼, making
the basis two cents.

In October, when Jason actually needed the corn,
market conditions had changed dramatically. The cash
corn price had risen to $2.26¼ per bushel from $2.23¼,
and Jason bought his requirements from local suppliers at
that higher price. He then lifted his hedge position by
selling his long positions in the futures market, where the
price had risen to $2.33 per bushel from $2.25¼. In retro-
spect, Jason's forecast that the basis was near its smallest
when it was two cents was very accurate. By October it
had risen to 6¾ cents.

All of which was very fortunate for him. On the hedge
position, Jason earned a profit of $694 (10,000 bushels
times 7¾ cents price appreciation in his long position
minus an $81 commission to his broker). "But in hedging

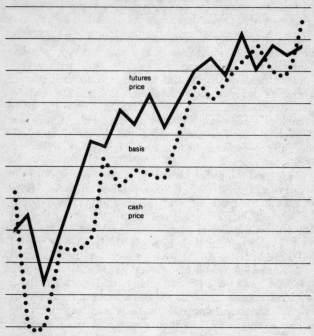

futures
price

basis

cash
price

The difference in cash prices and futures prices is known as the basis. (Chart by Chicago Board of Trade)

I'm really not looking to profit," he says. "I would be more than happy to just break even, because the protection I am getting against the big increases in cash prices are solace enough for me."

Yet hedgers like Jason realize profits far in excess of the numbers that show up on their brokerage accounts. In this particular case, for example, Jason says the hedge resulted in a tremendous savings in feed costs per heifer. "Per head, the hedge saved $2.21, and that added about 10 percent to the $20-per-head profit we usually make on each animal," he says.

The Fund Trader
("All for One, and One for All")

Andrew is a large man, more than six feet tall, weighing well over two hundred pounds and with the type of wide shoulders that you normally would associate with a professional football player. But he is not a football player, though he did play varsity football in college. Yet Andrew very much is involved in a team sport, for he is the quarterback of a commodity futures mutual fund. As such, he is solely responsible for making the decisions that will affect the investments of thousands of investors across the country.

It's a good thing that his shoulders are wide, because he is carrying a great deal of responsibility on them. "Running a fund is quite different from any other discipline in this market," he confides. "I can never lose sight of the fact that a great number of people are depending on my decisions. I have to treat their money with the utmost respect and consideration. And I have to consider their financial well-being when I make investment decisions."

Indeed, Andrew says that many fund managers have problems because they all too often make their decisions based on their own financial situations, and forget that the money is not theirs, but their clients'. "A fund manager generally is a successful, well-paid person who is making his own investments outside of his daily managing duties," Andrew says. "But those decisions can be based on his own wealth, family size, et cetera. If he starts to use those factors in making his decisions for the fund, problems can arise."

Andrew's sentiments about his concerns for his clients seem genuine, and that may set him apart from many of his colleagues in the fund-managing area. Another thing that sets him apart is the fact that his desk is not littered with computer printouts and the other paraphernalia one associates with investors employing technical analysis. Indeed, Andrew bases his decisions on fundamentals—supply-and-demand considerations—which sets him well apart from a world where most other fund managers employ technical analysis.

"Don't stick a computer in front of me," he jokes as he

sifts through the plethora of reports scattered across his desk. "I don't believe in them." Andrew says that, in his view anyway, computer analysis can be a "self-defeating waste of time." Why? "Most fund managers, and indeed big investors, rely on computers to signal buy and sell opportunities. And those signals all are predicated on basically the same set of rules, like five-day moving averages, twenty-day moving averages, and momentum techniques."

The problem with that, he says, is that everybody gets the same signals at approximately the same time. "As a result, there is a great potential for whipsawing—you know, where the trader ends up buying the highs and selling the lows. Who wants that?"

Instead, what Andrew does in trying to provide investors in his fund with profits is to seek out investments that fundamentally look strong over longer periods of time, such as twelve months down the road. During 1979, for example, his research pointed him in the direction of such metals as gold, silver, lead, and copper, as well as live cattle and rubber. "I gather all the data together that I can, then I take a long look down the road, and I make my move," he says, leaning back in his chair and putting his feet up on his desk. "I can take time to devote myself to my decisions to make sure that I am right. A technical analyst can't take the time to go to the men's room for fear that he will miss his market."

Though Andrew is adamantly in favor of the fundamental approach to futures analysis, he is the first to tell you that his method doesn't insure winners on each position assumed. In fact, his aim is to realize an equal number of winning and losing trades. By doing so and because of the leverage factor in futures that generally makes any winning position a huge winning position, he maintains he generally achieves his target of a 50 percent return annually on a noncumulative basis.

Another thing that he believes helps him achieve success is the degree of diversification that he builds into the fund with the various investments. For example, at any one time Andrew says his fund holds positions in ten to twelve different commodities so that investors are offered a healthy degree of protection. He structures it as follows:

· He never commits more than 15 percent of his fund's total resources to any one type of commodity.

· He maintains healthy cash and cash-equivalent reserves at all times so that he can act when the market is ready to move. For example, his commitment to the market generally runs from about 25 percent of the fund's assets to about 60 percent.

· He invests only in commodities which he feels give the fund's investors a profit potential of four times their possible loss. "Cattle is a good example of that," he says. "The nearest-term live-cattle contract currently is selling for 70.95 cents per pound. I think prices are going to fall because of oversupply. My research tells me that the upside risk is 72 cents and the downside potential is 66.75 cents. That meets my parameters and we took a position."

The Day Trader
("Rome Was Built in a Day")

Walt sleeps well at night. It wasn't always that way, however. That's because Walt is a day trader, a commodities futures market speculator who generally goes into and out of transactions all in the same day. He usually never carries a position overnight.

"When I walk out of the office at the end of the day, my mind is relatively clear," he says, while sipping a drink and glancing at the newspaper—the sports page—on the train home. "Oh, I still think about what I should have done differently during the day, or even what I may do tomorrow. But I sure as hell don't take my longs and my shorts home with me like I used to before I started day trading."

Though Walt may indeed be more relaxed than most futures traders when his working day is over, he nevertheless trades in a high-pressure atmosphere all day long. Trying to squeeze small profits out of quick entries and exits from the market requires not only a phenomenal understanding of the intricacies of the futures market but also a steady hand that can pull the trigger under fire.

Like most day traders, Walt is a follower, though in futures market parlance the term certainly does not have any derogatory connotations. "I'm not going to act until I see sufficient evidence that a breakout is underway," he says, setting the newspaper down on the empty seat next to his. "I tend to wait for a commodity to break out from a long-term consolidation, and then I buy or sell."

In doing so, Walt does not necessarily wait for prices to top out or bottom out before taking his profits. In profit-taking, at least, you'd probably want to call him a leader. "I don't want to wait for market tops or bottoms," he says. "I rely on gut feelings. When I feel that I have built up enough profits for just a quick venture, I get out. I'm not greedy."

By the same token, Walt maintains that a key for a day trader also is the ability to admit that he is wrong. "When a lot of guys see their positions heading south, they try to add to the losing positions so that they can average down," he says. "That's just a cop-out. More times than not it will make your losses greater. And, in any case, why tie up your funds in a losing proposition just to save face? If you are wrong, admit it, and try something else."

In monitoring the futures market, Walt likes to closely follow those contracts which trade together, because "when certain markets move in sympathy, it is quite easier to forecast the future." Indeed, he says he has predicted bull markets in sugar contracts on the basis of earlier upward movement in the metals markets.

When he is convinced that there is a bull market imminent in a specific commodity, Walt generally "lets it all fly." That is, he will invest heavily in that direction. "If I am convinced there is a big move coming, and I mean convinced, I'll put 90 percent of somebody's money into that one commodity," he says. And if that big move does materialize? "Well, I certainly don't just sit there and count up the paper profits." Indeed, Walt says, for those accounts which have been invested heavily into one commodity, he generally will take profits quickly and cut back the investors' exposure to the commodity to about 50 percent of total portfolio.

However, though he may trim back to 50 percent when he takes profits, Walt may also jump right back in later that same day. "You can't be afraid to be wrong in this business," he says, finishing his drink and ordering another. "If the market is still moving in the direction I want it to, I may jump right back in. I've flipped into and out of a market three times in one day."

While Walt follows all the markets fairly closely, he is especially fond of the trend markets such as currencies, grains, and precious metals like gold and silver, which generally undergo more consistent moves than do other types of currencies. "By sticking with those contracts," he says with a smile, "I've helped to put the odds a little more on my side."

Putting his newspaper under his arm, and standing up to leave, Walt smiles and begins to walk toward the train's door. "I may lose a million dollars tomorrow or I may make a million dollars, but that's tomorrow. Tonight I'm going to mow the lawn and then coach my Little League team. That's what is on my mind right now."

The Long-Term Trader
("Slow and Steady Is the Way")

There are at least sixty-five other people who work on the seventeenth floor of the Billings Building with Martin. You could bet the house that none of them has ever seen him with either his tie loosened or his jacket or vest removed. "I have a hard enough time getting him to take off his tie when he gets home," jokes his wife, Lois.

Martin believes that a successful businessman should look a certain way—and he does. Neat, trim, and always in control of everything. But that approach isn't just a facade that he limits to his appearance. Martin uses the same strict regimen in conducting his commodity trading activities. Everything must be under control, everything must be neat and trim, and every decision must be based on sound fundamental analysis. When he is satisfied, then he enters the market and waits for his decision to be verified by a move in the market.

Sometimes the move doesn't come for quite a while, however. Yet that doesn't bother Martin, because frequently he doesn't even check prices of contracts in which he holds a position for several days. That is because Martin is a long-term trader, basing his investment decisions on fundamentals, and as such in many cases is not interested in short-term fluctuations that may occur. "If the fundamentals are there, the expected price changes will follow. They have no choice," he says. "I'm not too concerned if prices don't go my way for a few days after I get into the market."

Sitting upright at a picnic table stationed on the patio in his backyard, Martin confesses that he doesn't follow every contract comprising the futures market. Instead, he says, he'll concentrate on a limited number—usually five —so that he'll never be surprised by an unanticipated event.

Being a fundamentalist, he generally is concerned with supply-and-demand considerations surrounding a commodity. "When it comes to agricultural commodities, the grains, foodstuffs, et cetera, most price moves are a result of a change in supply," he says. "Demand, for the most part, generally stays pretty constant. The only exception would be meat."

Shuffling through the stack of papers on the table in front of him, Martin explains how he views the prevailing cattle market. "The first thing I'm interested in is the long-term production cycle, say ten years long. When will the expansion begin and when will it end?" he says. "In addition, there also are several other measures that affect, and reflect, the cattle market: monthly slaughter, weekly slaughter, daily slaughter weight, the price of meats that compete with beef, the amount of meat available on a per-capita basis, the number of head available for slaughter, and the amount of income consumers have available to spend."

For example, he says, in the fall of 1978 he was long in the cattle market. "We knew we were entering a heavy liquidation phase and the key was when it was going to end," Martin says. "Fundamentally, the slaughter data was showing heavy culling of heifers and cows. Then, open interest began to fall quickly from the 100,000-contract mark, and then prices began to whipsaw. We decided to get out of the market at that point because it was obvious that consumers were beginning to rebel against the high prices of beef."

By the fall of 1979 Martin still was staying away from the cattle market. "The fundamentals aren't telling me anything right now," he says. "So I'm not going to rush into anything. When in doubt, stay out. There are right ways and wrong ways of doing things."

The Spreader
("Everything Is Relative")

Sit down at a party and strike up a conversation with Frank and you'll be terribly impressed with his knowledge. But you won't be terribly impressed with your own ability to figure out what Frank does for a living. That's because Frank is a highly intelligent man, whose scope of knowledge is wide-reaching, ranging from the number of pigs likely to be raised in Arkansas in two years to the relative merits of Teddy Kennedy or Jimmy Carter to the latest tax rules handed down by the Internal Revenue Service.

But while Frank's vast storage of knowledge may make it difficult for you to figure out what his Monday-through-Friday shtick is, that same databank in his head is what makes Frank such a success at what he does do: devise commodity spreads.

Indeed, one of the more sophisticated tools that a commodity trader uses is the spread, which also is known as straddle or switch. Simply put, a spread position attempts to take advantage of a change in relationship between prices on two contracts rather than a change in absolute value. In structuring a spread, therefore, a trader assumes both a buy, or long, and a sell, or short, position.

"In setting up a spread, I attempt to protect my client against catastrophic losses," says Frank. "But at the same time I try to structure the spread so that there still is the possibility of a percentage return on capital equal to that of outright long or short positions."

Because of the very nature of spread positions, therefore, the majority of Frank's clients are commercial concerns which seek the protection of spreads as an insurance policy against the vagaries of future price trends. Munching on a piece of chocolate candy that he received from a client, a candy company which plays the cocoa futures market, Frank adds that individuals also are being increasingly attracted to spreading as well. "The general public, particularly those investors with very small accounts, really like the spread," he says. "That's because spreads usually require smaller margin deposits than do regular transactions."

In entering spread transactions for both his customers

and for his own account, Frank can choose from four types of structures:

• Interdelivery Spread, which deals with two different delivery months of the same commodity on the same exchange.

• Intermarket Spread, which is the same commodity, and the same delivery month, but two different futures exchanges.

• Intercommodity Spread, which is two different, though generally related, commodities of the same delivery month on the same exchange.

• Source-Product Spread, which usually refers to the relationship between soybeans and its two products, soybean oil and soybean meal.

"For me, the interdelivery spread is used most often," says Frank, digging into the package for another piece of chocolate. "Primarily, that is because it is the least risky route to go."

When Frank is gearing up to structure an interdelivery spread, he attempts to anticipate changes that may occur in the relationship between the two sides of the spread. He buys the delivery month which he expects will rise in price and sells the delivery month which he feels will decline.

Interestingly, many interdelivery spreads are historical in nature and Frank tries to take advantage of them each year. "Generally, each year I'll go into four specific spreads: long May copper against short December copper; long June cattle against short October cattle; long July soybeans against short November soybeans; and long May corn against short July corn."

Frank also finds that straddle positions often recur in the intermarket area, specifically for wheat contracts traded on the Chicago Board of Trade, Kansas City Board of Trade, and Minneapolis Grain Exchange.

Despite the recurring nature of many of the spreads, analysis is extremely important in determining at which point to enter the market. "On the surface it seems that spreading should be easy, because many of the opportunities appear each year," Frank says. "But timing is extremely important. You still have to get into, and out of, your positions at the right time."

To reach those conclusions, then, Frank depends on four main areas of analysis; cyclic (seasonal); historical (price); fundamental (supply-demand); and technical (chart).

"The most important factor is the cyclic analysis as spreads tend to follow distinct seasonal patterns on a year-to-year basis regardless of short-term changes in supply and demand," he says. "This is due to recurring factors which are independent of the market; for example, the closing of Great Lakes shipping between December and April each year, which tends to act as a depressant on March grain contracts and as a stimulant to May grain deliveries."

Once Frank's analysis points out the contracts that should be included in his portfolio, he structures his endeavors with the four following guidelines, which have resulted in a 50 percent win performance over the years:

• "Never commit more than 20 percent of account equity to any one market.

• "Predefine risk and profit objectives before entering the trade.

• "If the risk is met—get out! Reanalyze the position and, if warranted, reenter, but do so from an unbiased position.

• "When predefined objectives are attained, take partial profits and raise your stop positions (or defined risk points) on the remaining positions to the entry point."

Of course, another important aspect of Frank's spread trading is to help his clients in the tax area. By setting up the positions in a certain way, long-term and short-term gains and losses can be manipulated so as to provide the client with the best possible tax benefits. "I may be a futures trader, but when you are a spreader you have to be a little bit of an accountant too," he says.

II. The Futures Market: A Word of Caution

When it comes to the futures markets, one thing is clear: Surging growth is the name of the game. And that growth is all the more evident when one examines what is happening in the United States' traditional financial marketplaces. Indeed, the stock and bond markets are being hit hard by the assault of soaring interest rates, a decade of runaway inflation, and economic uncertainty. Yet it is those features that are making the futures markets so attractive and helping them to grow so rapidly. Unfortunately, in the view of many people, the futures markets may be part of the cause of those conditions as well.

To be sure, the futures markets are attracting a wide variety of investors, individual and institutional, domestic and foreign. Why? It is because of the small margins, or initial down payments, required and the vast array of trading vehicles from which an investor can choose in his attempt to beat inflation. Yet, a phenomenon troubling to many critics of the markets is the charge that the massive growth in futures may be draining huge sums of money away from the traditional capital-formation mainstream that is so necessary to this country's well-being. That is, money that investors might instead invest in stocks and thus make available to corporate America is instead going into the futures marketplace, which in reality deals in nothing more than paper contracts. But, because stocks and bonds are not offering the types of returns that are necessary to attract investors, the money continues to go into futures. Says an executive of one of the U.S.'s largest futures exchanges: "The more uncertainty, the more business. As human beings and citizens, we deplore the state of the economy. But the state is good for business."

To the futures industry's credit, however, investors' growing thirst for an investing medium capable of doing battle with inflation has not gone unnoticed. Indeed, new types of products such as financial instrument futures and new exchanges such as the Amex Commodity Exchange (ACE) and New York Futures Exchange (NYFE) unit of the New York Stock Exchange are being developed as quickly as possible as those involved in the industry try to capture a larger piece of the $1.4 trillion and still-growing futures pie.

Consider, for a moment, the growth the various exchanges have enjoyed (see chart on p. 37).

Yet, this phenomenal growth is not occurring without criticism, and any investor considering the futures market should be aware of the charges. For example, it is a statistical fact that the majority of futures traders lose money on most of their transactions. Yet the payoffs in the futures market are so lucrative that an occasional big win keeps that same investor coming back despite the frequent losses. The trouble is, industry critics contend, many of the sophisticated futures traders realize the high risks involved and can deal with them more effectively than the more naive traders who currently are flocking to the markets. Moreover, they add, many of the newer players in the futures game are investors who are more familiar with stocks and bonds than futures and therefore too often take long positions, or those expecting rises in prices, because of their greater familiarity with stocks.

As a result, many critics maintain that the industry may be growing too fast. And this, they charge, is extra disturbing because of the difficulties the Commodity Futures Trading Commission has had in keeping up with the markets. In fact, say many critics, the CFTC has been a dismal failure in carrying out its mandate to regulate the thriving futures markets.

Number of Contracts Traded

Exchange	1974	1975	1976	1977	1978	Est. 1979
Chicago Board of Trade	14,557,435	15,942,066	18,895,156	23,019,825	27,362,929	40,495,136
Chicago Mercantile Exchange	5,293,880	6,401,956	6,201,665	7,878,247	15,153,952	24,602,686
Commodity Exchange Inc.	1,779,805	3,789,937	5,464,282	5,591,808	8,973,828	18,048,780
Amex Commodities Exchange					16,671	42,264
Kansas City Board of Trade	426,694	608,901	688,350	617,137	755,949	832,396
MidAmerica Commodity Exchange	2,572,848	2,414,621	2,231,866	2,066,195	2,121,189	3,295,920
Minneapolis Grain Exchange	178,562	199,365	228,555	191,134	284,313	292,109
New York Cocoa Exchange	345,264	317,960	334,032	307,681	222,732	195,745
New York Coffee & Sugar Exchange	932,429	873,068	1,173,228	1,285,862	1,202,607	1,760,756
New York Cotton Exchange	518,048	630,935	1,017,966	1,204,620	1,441,209	2,070,609
New York Mercantile Exchange	1,008,470	1,006,803	640,115	684,555	926,793	952,720
Pacific Commodity Exchange	20,349	14,491	1,512			
West Coast Commodity Exchange	19,544					
Total contracts	27,733,328	32,200,103	36,876,727	42,880,318	58,462,172	92,589,121
Percentage increase from previous year	+7.37%	+16.11%	+14.52%	+16.3%	+36.3%	+58.4%

Thus, despite the spectacular growth that has marked the futures industry over the years, especially in the inflation-marred decade of the 1970s, a dark cloud hangs over the industry. And that cloud contains the following elements:

• Charges that trading in the futures market is not always predicated on actual supply-and-demand considerations. Thus, critics say, spot prices of the physical commodity may undergo futures market-induced movements that are not warranted and which thus may well be inflationary.

• Criticism that many U.S. corporations are being robbed of their ability to raise necessary capital because of the growing volume of cash that the futures markets are drawing away from stocks and bonds.

• Allegations that, because of their desire to capitalize on the phenomenal growth in futures, many exchanges are creating futures contracts that have absolutely no economic justification.

• Mounting questions as to whether the CFTC is able to regulate these markets or whether they should be placed under the jurisdiction of the more established and certainly more powerful Securities and Exchange Commission, which oversees the stock markets.

Ironically, one of the most troubling areas also is one of the fastest-growing. Indeed, not only are the financial instrument futures generating criticism from within the industry, but they also are catching a great deal of flack from outside as well, especially from the Securities and Exchange Commission. For one thing, many officials at the SEC feel that the huge sums of money that are being drawn into futures are severely impacting the United States' capital-raising abilities.

Moreover, many critics also charge that the shoot-from-the-hip futures markets are having an adverse impact on the spot prices of the underlying commodities. Rep. Neil Smith, a Democratic congressman from Iowa, is one of those critics. As chairman of the House Small Business Committee, Smith, at the time of this writing, had begun investigating charges that the large meat-packing firms of this country have attempted to control beef prices so as to profit from positions they have taken in the beef futures markets.

Smith's fears appear well founded. Consider the wisdom of my favorite futures market oracle, whom I've nick-named Freddie the Lip. "If I'm a top officer at a company that supplies any necessary product, whether it's meat, potatoes, or whatever, I have an advantage over everybody else who is trying to play the market," he says. "I know when spot prices are going to go up or down because there is too little or too much meat. And I also know when prices are going to go up or down when there is no reason at all. If I know those things, then I have an almost foolproof idea of what futures prices are going to do as well."

The charge that futures are having a detrimental effect on the prices of underlying commodities also has made its way to the financial futures area, where both the U.S. Treasury Department and the Federal Reserve System have expressed concerns that the futures markets for U.S. Treasury instruments could adversely affect the United States' ability to offer debt securities by artificially raising interest rates. Yet, in a joint study, the two agencies concluded that the futures contracts were not that bad after all.

Ironically, the growth of financial futures has been spurred by just the type of economic woes many feel the instruments may cause. Indeed, uncertain economic conditions, vacillating currencies and the runaway inflation of the 1970s surely were the catalysts that created the spectacular financial futures markets.

The Chicago Mercantile Exchange (CME), the nation's second-largest futures mart, was the first exchange to recognize that the changing economic circumstances were fodder for the new financial instruments. In 1972 the Merc established a market for futures contracts on various foreign currencies, such as the widely followed Japanese yen and West German mark.

Then, in October 1975 the giant Chicago Board of Trade (CBOT) got into the act, when it began trading contracts on Government National Mortgage Association bonds. The Chicago Merc followed with Treasury bills and the CBOT countered with new contracts on Treasury bonds and commercial paper.

In 1978 some new players, with very familiar names, started to get into the game. In September, for example, the Amex Commodity Exchange started up with contracts on the, by-then, already popular Ginnie Mae futures.

By this time the floodgates already were wide open as the other various stock and futures exchanges around the country could see how popular the new instruments were with the investing public. The New York Stock Exchange, the world's largest securities market, let it be known that it wanted in, either via a merger with an existing futures market or through the start-up of its own market. And, also in New York, the Commodity Exchange Inc. (Comex), a successful exchange dealing primarily in precious metals, also announced plans for an expansion into financial futures as well as a West Coast satellite office.

But despite these aggressive marketing efforts, the charges continue that futures market activities have moved away from the traditional supply-and-demand mainstream. Indeed, prices of grain futures traded in Chicago are used to arrange grain transactions throughout the world. And, in some cases, the power and clout of the futures market may well be escalating. Copper producers, for example, have begun to tie the price of that metal to futures market quotes. And industry officials concede that this practice tends to make the copper market more volatile as well as pushes prices higher.

These concerns, then, are causing many market critics to point an accusing finger at the federal CFTC, which they say has been lax in regulating the market. Indeed, in any business that moves as quickly and involves as much money as the futures market, regulation is an extremely important question. And, unfortunately, the futures industry has over the years picked up a reputation as a rather undisciplined and unregulated marketplace. Quite simply, some of that reputation is deserved. The futures markets have been hit with numerous scandals and attempts at market manipulation by traders or firms. Yet, in many ways the scandals are no more serious than many that have affected the stock and bond markets, or which have touched other businesses, such as banking.

Perhaps the industry's reputation has been hurt most because of the lack of a regulator capable of overseeing its burgeoning growth. Indeed, the basic premise of the commodities futures industry is that exchanges generally regulate themselves. And, years ago, that did prove difficult on several occasions. For example, a trader at a certain futures exchange would be accused of some infraction by a customer, and that charge would be passed along to the exchange's board of governors or some other exchange committee charged with enforcement. In many cases, however, that same trader would be a member of the committee or board, or the members would be friends or associates of that trader. Because of those cases, it is not hard to understand why the industry picked up such a poor reputation for regulation.

Federally, regulation was under the jurisdiction of the Commodity Exchange Authority, a branch of the United States Department of Agriculture. The CEA was clearly a weak sister that had absolutely no muscle in either the surveillance or enforcement areas.

However, the United States Congress recognized that the market needed a strong regulator to oversee the expected surging growth, and in 1974 took steps to do just that. In 1975 the fledgling Commodity Futures Trading Commission was set up as a separate entity with jurisdiction over all futures exchanges operating in this country, the trading of commodity options, and the trading of gold and silver leverage contracts. Its mandate is quite clear: to insure honest practices in futures trading and to regulate activities which may hurt the integrity of a free market or which may harm the marketplace or its users.

Said the Senate Committee on Agriculture and Forestry in November 1974:

The futures market is a very important part of our economy, providing an indispensable tool for agricultural producers, exporters and consumers. In order to assure that futures markets operate properly and that the prices consumers pay are not artificially high, careful and efficient supervision of the markets is essential. The proper regulatory function is to assure that the market is free from manipulation and other practices which prevent the market from being a true reflection of supply and demand.

Yet the CFTC has encountered some rocky roads since

its inception, and even today is regarded as one of Washington's softest regulators. Moreover, the commission has been hurt greatly over the years by numerous vacancies at its top positions, a naive staff, and a budget that was far too small. "Unlike the SEC, the CFTC has never had a clear vision of its mission," states Beverly J. Splane, a former CFTC staff official and now executive vice president of the Chicago Mercantile Exchange.

However, in 1979 the commission got off to what many observers hoped was a fresh new start when a new chairman was named. The former insurance commissioner from Massachusetts, James M. Stone, replaced William T. Bagley as head of the agency and brought with him a reputation as a very strict regulator.

Yet, despite the fresh start that the naming of Stone was supposed to give the agency, the CFTC continued to encounter problems. For example, in early spring of 1979 four traders on the Chicago Board of Trade aggregated futures positions totaling nearly 7.5 million bushels of wheat. At the same time, however, just 2 million bushels of actual wheat were on hand in Chicago.

As a result, the CFTC, believing that such developments raised the possibility of a squeeze, tried to suspend trading. Probably as a result of the commission's poor reputation, however, the CBOT would not sit still for such a move and countered by filing a suit against the agency. Surprisingly, when the case went to court, the CFTC refused to present testimony in support of its action and the judge in the case found in favor of the exchange. Apparently, sources contend, the agency attempted to "play hardball" in the case and persuade the judge that it didn't need to present evidence in such a proceeding because of its charter as the federal regulator of the markets. Obviously, the strategy backfired, and the commission's image was dealt another severe blow.

But for the individual investors who are flocking to the market as a way to do battle with double-digit inflation, these political issues hold very little significance. Indeed, performance of the various contracts and growth of the market is of utmost importance to them. But that surging growth is not limited solely to the new smaller players coming into the game, for more and more large institutions—banks, pension-fund managers, and securities dealers—also are running willy-nilly to futures. For example, consider the case of Community First Bank of Bakersfield, California. That institution has been hedging its investment portfolio since 1977 by using futures contracts in instruments such as Ginnie Mae and Treasury bonds. And that strategy has worked out very well. In 1978, for instance, the bank earned $642,000 from its hedging activities.

This surging interest in futures also is proving to be a bonanza for the brokerage industry. Indeed, since May 1, 1975, the securities industry has been forced to contract sharply because of the freeing of fixed brokerage commission rates, an event that dried up a great deal of the firms' revenues. As a result, they have actively been looking for new revenues sources, and futures have nicely filled that need. In 1978, for example, futures commissions of New York Stock Exchange member firms totaled $351 million, or 8.5 percent of total industry commissions of $4.1 billion. That was an increase of nearly 33 percent in just four years. It's obvious, then, that more and more firms are likely to attempt to get a piece of the business. "Commodities are no longer what they used to be," says Perrin H. Long, Jr., an analyst with Lipper Analytical Distributors Inc. in New York. "The annual compound rate of change between 1972 and 1978 is 19.6 percent for futures revenues, compared to 6.7 percent for total industry revenues. Everybody is gearing up internally."

The importance of futures revenues should not be understated. The raging success of one of the first full-service firms that got into futures heavily, Shearson Loeb Rhoades Inc., is a perfect example. Once a small firm, Shearson today ranks as the nation's second-largest brokerage house and in 1978 garnered about 33 percent, or $44.3 million, of its total revenues of $136.7 million from futures brokerage. "It's a growing market. As more and more people get educated about futures, it will grow even more and be an even greater factor for our business," says Shearson's chairman and president, Sanford I. Weill.

Yet market critics contend that such an offensive by the securities industry may well be luring unsuspecting and naive investors into a very dangerous game. One charge is

that the birth of managed accounts is causing many speculators to attempt to trade futures without learning how to
first. Of course, in a managed account, an investor grants
power of attorney to his broker, who then makes all the
buy-and-sell decisions. The same critics also say that futures mutual funds, or pools, also are pulling in the unsuspecting novice.

These charges are generating a great deal of concern. "I
am afraid that too much unknowledgeable speculation can
be detrimental," says Robert K. Wilmouth, president of
the Chicago Board of Trade. "There is a point where it
becomes dangerous with people who don't understand
what they are doing. With great leverage, they have fantastic (profit) opportunities. But they have fantastic opportunities for loss."

And while the managed accounts and mutual funds still
are relatively new aspects of the futures markets, critics
also contend that, much like in the stock market, these
new large "institutional investors" are causing an already
volatile market to become even more volatile. And that, in
turn, makes the futures market an even riskier proposition
for those unsophisticated investors.

Meanwhile, the march onward continues, with exchanges proposing several new types of contracts, especially in the financial futures area, and with the possibility
of commodity options also being listed on this country's
futures exchanges. The plethora of new proposals includes
plans for contracts on leaded and unleaded gasoline as well
as one extremely interesting, albeit highly criticized, plan
by the Kansas City Board of Trade. That exchange has
designed a contract that would be tied to the Value Line
Composite Index, which is based on the prices of more than
sixteen hundred stocks.

The plan is unique in several aspects because it specifies
cash settlements of all contracts since there are no actual
deliverable supplies. As a result, critics are charging that
such a contract is ignoring the premise on which the futures market was born—supply and demand. "The risk
we run there is in settlement for cash," says a high-ranking
official of another exchange. "I'm not certain that that
does not bring us very close to the gambling aspect. That
bothers me."

And that gambling aspect is surely the one thing with

which futures markets proponents do not want their business associated. So to you novice investors, remember at all times that any financial marketplace is only as good as its components. So, when you go out to do battle with inflation, be careful. Futures can both help you and harm you.

III. The Futures Market: What You Need to Know to Play

THE ORIGINS

Considering the rapidly changing economies that mark the world today, it is somewhat surprising the number of investors who are flocking to an investment medium as old as the futures market. The ranks include sophisticated professionals who know the angles, large institutions such as banks which have the financial clout, and small unsophisticated individuals who are looking for a way to beat rampant inflation.

Indeed, if one wanted to trace the concept of futures trading back to its origins, one would find that its principles and functions are nearly as old as civilization itself. The "trading markets" that took root in many an ancient dusty street clearly centered on the exchange of goods and currencies, the setting of fixed prices, and the anticipation of price trends and production costs.

While loosely organized and certainly not regulated, these early exchanges flourished, and eventually found their way across the Atlantic Ocean from Europe into the wilderness that ultimately would become America. By the late 1700s, just as the new country was beginning to take shape and become the vibrant and wealthy entity it is, so too were the neophyte futures exchanges that would grow and mature into the markets that constitute today's futures industry.

For an investor who wished to play the commodity markets in those times, the process would have been a great deal simpler, however. In New York, for example, the investor would have found easy access to markets that provided him the opportunity to take financial positions in such commodities as grain, butter, eggs, or a variety of vegetables. Yet, even then, the markets were primarily "spot" or "cash" markets dealing in prices that prevailed at the time of delivery.

But as the markets grew bigger, and the number of farmers and merchants involved in them also climbed, it became apparent that a system more sophisticated than the traditional one of spot pricing was necessary. For example, supplies of a various product such as grain would be scarce in a given year due to weather conditions, and the farmers would reap a huge financial reward from the merchants who bid up the grain prices in their burning desire to get the product they needed. Conversely, when supplies were plentiful, the grain merchants would keep their bids low, and even those farmers who were lucky enough to have their crops bid on would oftentimes receive payments far smaller than the amount of money that they had invested in growing the crops. And those who didn't receive bids at all frequently were forced to leave their crops in the street, on the railcar, or even on the boat and turn around and head back to their farms penniless.

Those developments had real significance because they signaled the maturation of the supply-and-demand forces that are the backbone of today's futures markets. It was evident, as these problems mounted, that a better system was needed. At first, farmers and merchants started on their own and began to make contracts that specified prices and amounts for future delivery. Ultimately, this feeble attempt at self-protection mushroomed, and formal futures exchanges began to surface in various cities. The Chicago Board of Trade (CBOT), for example, which today is this nation's largest and best-known futures exchange, was the first to surface, making its debut in 1848.

Though the industry made remarkable strides in organization as the nineteenth century wound its way to a close, the markets still were rather undisciplined arenas

The Chicago Board of Trade (CBOT) has had numerous homes since its birth in 1848. This facility housed the exchange between 1894 and 1928. (Photo by Chicago Board of Trade)

that were treaded only by the knowledgeable few. Things are different today, however, and the futures markets are far from being just marketplaces for farmers, grain merchants, or cash-laden speculators. Schoolteachers from Des Moines, truck drivers from Memphis, and retired dentists from Duluth all are utilizing the futures markets.

The growth has been so phenomenal, in fact, that it is hard to believe. Consider the following table, detailing the value of futures traded on all United States exchanges:

Year	Billions of dollars
1969	$108.3
1970	145.3
1971	172.2
1972	257.7
1973	520.1
1974	571.6
1975	597.6
1976	819.1
1977	1,100.0
1978	1,430.0

Data: Commodity Futures Trading Commission

Why has the growth been so sharp? Quite simply, the futures game has clearly become the only game in town for individuals and institutions looking for a way to fight back against the runaway inflation that is eating away at their earnings and savings. The traditional games—stocks, bonds, savings accounts—have been rendered unworkable in such an environment. Stock prices with the exception of various nooks and crannies of the market are moving sideways, and as a whole are being dwarfed by inflation. Bonds, while generally presenting nice yields with great safety, do not promise capital appreciation. And money stashed away in savings accounts, especially for individuals who are years away from retirement, is money that simply is not being put to work.

As a result, more and more money and people are being drawn into futures. The chance for big profits is evident (as is the chance for huge losses) and in most cases the amount of money needed to trade a contract is relatively small compared with the size of the position it will purchase. But as more and more new players enter the game, the game becomes more volatile. And a volatile game clearly benefits the experienced player more than it aids the novice.

For those reasons, it is imperative that anyone considering a venture into the futures markets should educate himself as much as possible on what the markets are all about. Trading strategies which can be quite elaborate must be understood, risks and rewards must be determined, and where to go and who to ask for help must be part of one's everyday working knowledge. For at all times an investor must remember that he is using his money, and not his broker's, or the farmer's. And in most cases, the investor is the one who is best able to look out for his own interests.

A woman in her late sixties went through a harrowing experience a few years back. On the advice of her broker, she had invested $10,000 in futures on the expectation that prices were going to rise. They didn't and she was required to put up additional funds (margin) to maintain her position. When told that prices had gone against her, she asked her broker why he hadn't told her while it was happening. She was informed that prices are printed daily in various newspapers (such as *The Wall Street Journal*) and also broadcast over numerous radio and television stations during the course of a trading day. She replied: "I didn't know that."

The example may well be extreme, but it does happen. And because it does, and so that it doesn't happen too much in the future, the following is offered.

HOW TO OPEN AN ACCOUNT

The first rule of thumb: Shop for a brokerage house to do business with in much the same way you would look for a doctor. Seek out referrals, check out track records, and take the time to have a good long conversation with the broker before you give him any of your money to invest in the futures market.

While the second rule of thumb is not always 100 percent foolproof, it nevertheless is a good practice to do your business with a firm that has a proven record of operation, and has a reputation that it isn't about to compromise for one small account—yours. For commodity futures accounts your safest bets are six firms: Merrill Lynch, Pierce, Fenner & Smith Inc., Shearson Loeb Rhoades Inc., E.F. Hutton & Co., Bache Halsey Stuart Shields Inc., ContiCommodity Services Inc. and Clayton Brokerage Co. of St. Louis. All have been involved in serving individual investors interested in futures for many years and all are big enough to provide you with both the safety and the research expertise that you require.

Remember, advising clients on how to invest in commodity futures and how to invest in stocks and bonds are sharply different disciplines. An account executive for one firm may have an excellent record for one of your neighbors in turning profits on his stock portfolio, but that doesn't mean that he knows the difference between a pork belly and a Ginnie Mae future. Ask him about his record. If he balks, you know that he isn't the one you want.

I can speak to these problems first-hand. In researching this book I decided that it would be useful to put a few brokers through tests, not only to determine how competent they were, but also to ascertain their ethics. My phone call to the very first one on my list is a good lesson in Investing 101:

MLG: I'd like some information on opening up an account.

Broker: Fine, just let me get a form to fill out. (He got the form, and took down the necessary information, name, address, Social Security number, etc.) Where do you work?

MLG: McGraw-Hill, for *Business Week* magazine.

Broker: Oh really? What area do you write about?

MLG: Investing. Listen, can I trade both stocks and futures through you?

Broker: Absolutely, this is a full-service firm.

MLG: Great, what do you think about Schlumberger stock?

Broker: Just a second, let me look it up to see what our analysts think. . . . Earnings are good. It looks like it will have a pretty good run. Would you like me to put in an order?

MLG: Just a second, I'm not sure. I'd much rather hit the futures market at this point. How does stud lumber look to you? Supplies look scarce and I think prices are going to rise.

Broker: Stud lumber? Uh . . . Uh . . . Well, I'll tell you what. You sound like you've done your homework on that. This is what I suggest. Let me put in your order for the stud-lumber futures, and then I'll call our futures people in Chicago to get their views. I'll call you back in a few days and let you know what they say.

CLAYTON BROKERAGE CO. of St. Louis, Inc.
Suite 300 ● 7701 Forsyth Blvd. ● St. Louis, Mo. 63105 ● 314-727-8000 ● Telex: 447201 CBCO CLAY

CONTACT
SHEET

Name _____ Soc. Sec.# _____ Age _____

Address _____ City _____ State _____ Zip _____

Home Address (if different) _____ City _____ State _____ Zip _____

Phone (Home) _____ Phone (Business) _____

Employer's Name _____ Address _____

City _____ State _____ Zip _____

Position Title _____ How Long at Present Job _____ Citizenship _____

Spouse's Name _____ Spouse's Employment _____ Part Time _____ Full Time _____

Principal Bank and Address _____ Acct.# _____

Annual Income: ☐ Less than $12,000   ☐ $12,000 to $25,000   ☐ $25,000 to $50,000   ☐ More than $50,000

Liquid Net Worth: ☐ Less than $20,000   ☐ $20,000 to $50,000   ☐ $50,000 to $100,000   ☐ More than $100,000

Other Net Worth: $ _____ Real Estate: $ _____

Will account be traded on your behalf by anyone else?   ☐ Yes   ☐ No

If yes, please identify trader and attach power of attorney _____

Indicate Type of Account:

   ☐ Individual   ☐ Partnership   ☐ Corporation   ☐ Joint Tenancy   ☐ Tenants in Common   ☐ Trust   ☐ Other

Account Source:

   ☐ Walk-in   ☐ Referral   ☐ Adv./Mailing   ☐ Conv./Seminar   ☐ Personal   ☐ Other _____

Indicate whether account will be used for ☐ Hedging or ☐ Speculation

Do you currently, or did you in the past have commodity accounts with Clayton or any other commodity brokerage firm? ☐ Yes ☐ No

If yes, please identify account _____

Have you ever had an unsecured debit at any other brokerage firm?   ☐ Yes   ☐ No

Are you related to any Clayton Brokerage employees?   ☐ Yes   ☐ No

If yes, please identify employee and relationship _____

Are you a member of the Chicago Board of Trade, the Chicago Mercantile Exchange,

or any other commodities exchange?   ☐ Yes   ☐ No

If yes, please identify exchange(s) _____

Investment Experience	No	Yes	Since (Year)	Do you understand:	Yes	No
Stocks and Bonds	☐	☐	_____	Basics of Commodity Futures Trading	☐	☐
Stock Options	☐	☐	_____	Risk of Loss & Debit Balance	☐	☐
Funds	☐	☐	_____	That your transactions will be made only with		
Commodity Futures	☐	☐	_____	prior verbal or written authorization	☐	☐

Initial Deposit: $ _____

TO THE BEST OF MY KNOWLEDGE, THE ABOVE APPLICATION IS TRUE AND CORRECT

_____   _____   _____   _____
Customer's signature   Date   RCR's signature   Date

Bank reference checked with _____ By _____

On _____ With _____
      Date   Comments

Office Manager Review/Date _____ Home Office Review/Date _____

In opening up an account, a customer will have to fill out a variety of forms, including one such as that used by Clayton Brokerage Co. of St. Louis.

AUTHORIZATION TO TRANSFER FUNDS

Gentlemen:

Without limiting or modifying the general provisions of the above Agreement with you, you are hereby specifically authorized, until further notice in writing, to transfer from my Regulated Commodity Account to my Unregulated Commodity Account such amount of excess funds as in your judgement may be necessary at any time to avoid the calling of margins in my open trades in unregulated commodity futures, or to reduce the debit balance in said account. By "Regulated Commodity" is meant any commodity futures contract sold or purchased on a Contract Market as that term is defined in the Commodity Exchange Act, as amended. This authorization is conditioned upon your prompt confirmation in writing of any and all transfers of funds made pursuant hereto.

_____

Date _____   _____

Signature(s) of Customer(s)

DECLARATIONS OF INTEREST

(The following forms of declaration are made available for Customer's Agreements signed by two or more individuals who desire to define their individual interests in accounts established under this Agreement. The interests hereby disclosed constitute full ownership of the accounts. In the event a signatory is a partnership or corporation, a separate resolution or authorization is required.)

DECLARATION OF JOINT TENANCY

To: Clayton Brokerage Co. of St. Louis, Inc.

The account or accounts held pursuant to the preceding Customer's Agreement are hereby declared to be held as joint tenants, and not as tenants in common by _____ and _____ Balances in such account or accounts may be paid to either of the aforesaid during the lifetime of both, or to the survivor after the death of one of them. It is understood and agreed that payment made to either party pursuant to the preceding sentence shall be a valid and sufficient release and discharge to Clayton Brokerage Co. of St. Louis, Inc., whether any of the parties be living or dead, for all obligations owing from Clayton Brokerage Co. of St. Louis, Inc. on such account or accounts. It is further agreed that Clayton Brokerage Co. of St. Louis, Inc. may insist upon a certified copy of the death certificate of one of the parties before making payment of the balance in such account or accounts to the survivor.

It is further understood and agreed that the obligations of the above as owners of the account or accounts held pursuant to the preceding Customer's Agreement are joint and several. In all matters pertaining to the account, Clayton Brokerage Co. of St. Louis, Inc. may act upon orders and instructions from any of the undersigned.

_____

DECLARATION OF INTEREST HELD AS TENANTS IN COMMON

To: Clayton Brokerage Co. of St. Louis, Inc.

The undersigned hereby declare that the account or accounts held pursuant to the preceding Customer's Agreement are held as tenants in common. The share of each of the undersigned in the aforesaid account or accounts shall be determined in accordance with the percentage of ownership set forth below. You shall have no obligation with respect to your handling of this account in the event of the death of one of the undersigned other than on receipt of actual notice of the death of one of the undersigned to take as expeditiously as possible such action as may be possible to reduce the account to a cash position by the closing of all outstanding futures transactions which you are hereby specifically authorized to do.

Notwithstanding this declaration, it is understood and agreed that the obligations of the undersigned as an owner of the account or accounts held pursuant to the preceding Customer's Agreement are joint and several. In all matters pertaining to the account, Clayton Brokerage Co. of St. Louis, Inc. may act upon orders and instructions from any of the undersigned.

_____ Ownership _____ %

_____ Ownership _____ %

_____ Ownership _____ %

MLG: Don't you keep up-to-date on the futures market?

Broker: Sure, absolutely. It's just that we have other guys who follow the market full-time, and they know more about it than I do.

MLG: Oh, I see.

Broker: Listen, let's put the order in and see where it goes.

While my own experience could be the exception to the rule, it is nevertheless indicative of the risks that we all run when considering investments in anything as fast moving as futures. You must set up the standards under which you will operate and never deviate from them.

Moreover, at all times resist those firms that approach you over the telephone or through the mail. While the firm may save you money in commissions or administrative costs, the risk you run is far greater than the savings involved. If the firm has to approach you blindly over the phone or through the mail, it probably is not doing enough business based on its performance record to keep its head above water.

How you structure your account is your choice, of course, but basically you can do it in three ways: individually, jointly with an associate, or in the name of your company. Before entering into a joint account, however, first realize that only one member of the group can be responsible for ordering transactions. If you have some problem with that type of setup, look into a different structure. In addition, you may elect to join a futures pool or mutual fund, in which you own shares in a pool of money that is being invested in a variety of futures, or you may choose to set up a futures managed account, in which you sign over power of attorney to your broker, who then conducts all your trades. Those two types of investing choices will be dealt with later in this chapter.

WHAT TYPES OF ORDERS YOU CAN PLACE

Once you have decided which firm and which account executive you want to do business with, it is time to take to the market. If you have decided to eschew the managed-fund and mutual-fund approaches, you and your broker should be working hand in hand to reach your investment decisions. When you have decided on the specific market positions you wish to take, you then will have two basic options on how to place your orders:

· Market Orders: In entering a market order with a broker, a customer declares how many contracts in a specific commodity he wishes to buy or sell. However, similar to an "at-the-market" transaction with stocks, the customer does not specify at which price he wants the order consummated, only that it should be done as quickly as possible at the prevailing market price.

· Contingency Orders: In entering a contingency order a customer is placing much stricter parameters on the nature of his trade. In addition to the volume and month specified in the market order, a customer utilizing contingency orders also may specify price and time guidelines in which his ordered trade should be transacted.

Moreover, within the framework of contingency orders rest several types of price and time restrictions that not only are designed to maximize the possible profit you may accrue, but also which can protect your interests in the event of sharp market movements. They are:

· Stop Orders: Traditionally, stop orders are used to cut losses on earlier transactions though they also may be utilized in maximizing profits. For example, a customer may buy 25,000 pounds of December copper for 83.30 cents a pound and simultaneously enter a stop order at 82.20 cents. If that lower price level is hit, the position is liquidated and the customer has cut his losses before they can become deeper. Of course, had the price of copper risen to 86.30 cents at some time after his purchase at 83.30 cents, the customer could then have entered a stop order for 85.30 cents, thus insuring that he did profit from the transaction.

· Fill or Kill Orders: These specify that an order must be executed at a specified price and only at that price. If, for example, the broker cannot fill the order after three attempts, the fill or kill order provides that the order be cancelled.

· Market If Touched Orders: These orders specify a specific price. When that price is reached the order is automatically activated.

· Day Orders: These orders restrict execution to a specified price reached during a single-day period.

· Good Till Cancelled Orders: These are long-standing orders which are alive until the specified price is reached or until the contract is cancelled.

WHAT ABOUT POOLS OR MUTUAL FUNDS?

As the futures markets have become more and more attractive to small investors over the past few years as a way to fight inflation, the futures industry has responded by working hard to develop new ways to open the doors to the markets so that this new breed of speculator could enter. The managed account, which generally requires initial investments ranging from as little as a few thousand dollars to as much as $50,000, was the first step. In the past few years, however, the door has been opened wider with the creation of commodity futures pools, or mutual funds, which allow investors willing to put up as little as $5,000 to obtain managed and diversified positions in the futures market.

More and more of these pools are springing up every day, and by some measures more than $50 million of small investors' funds are being managed in such a manner. One caveat, however: Though stock mutual funds have over the years developed the reputation as very safe harbors of investors' money, futures mutual funds carry the same risk characteristics as do futures which are traded individually. For example, the prospectus detailing a futures fund always carries the following warning attached to it:

RISK DISCLOSURE STATEMENT

You should carefully consider whether your financial condition permits you to invest in the partnership (fund). You may lose a substantial porition or even all of such investment.

In considering whether to invest, you should be aware that trading commodity contracts can quickly

Preliminary Prospectus Dated March 30, 1979

5,000 Units of Limited Partnership Interest

McLEAN FUTURES FUND II

McLean Futures Fund II (the "Partnership") is a limited partnership organized to engage in speculative trading of futures contracts in commodities (including treasury bills, other financial instruments and foreign currencies). ContiCommodity Services, Inc. ("Conti") is the Partnership's commodity broker and Conti's subsidiary, Fairfax Management Company, is the General Partner. See "Conflicts of Interest and Responsibility of the General Partner" and "The General Partner and the Commodity Broker." All trading decisions are made by Chowanoc Management Company, Inc. (the "Trading Manager"). See "The Trading Manager." The Units are offered at $1,000 per Unit. The minimum subscription is $5,000. Although the Units are transferable, no market exists for their sale and none is likely to develop. Units may, however, be redeemed monthly at Net Asset Value on 15 days' written notice less 10% of such Net Asset Value in the case of redemptions occurring during the 12 month period after the Partnership commences trading activities. See "Redemptions." The General Partner has sole discretion as to the distribution of profits, if any, of the Partnership. See "Federal Income Tax Aspects."

The Units of Limited Partnership Interest ("Units") of the Partnership are being offered through Conti-Securities, Inc. and Wheat, First Securities, Inc. (the "Selling Agents") on a best efforts basis without any firm underwriting commitment for 45 days from the date hereof, subject to an extension for up to an additional 30 days at the General Partner's discretion, unless all Units have previously been subscribed for. Funds paid by subscribers will be deposited in an escrow account with Harris Trust and Savings Bank and, if subscriptions for at least 2,000 Units have not been received within such period, such funds will be promptly returned with any interest earned thereon. If subscriptions for 2,000 or more Units have been received within such period, the Partnership may accept such subscriptions and commence trading activities. See "Plan of Distribution" and "Subscription Procedure."

THE BUSINESS OF THE PARTNERSHIP AND THESE SECURITIES INVOLVE A HIGH DEGREE OF RISK. THESE SECURITIES ARE SUITABLE FOR INVESTMENT ONLY BY A PERSON WHO CAN AFFORD TO LOSE HIS ENTIRE INVESTMENT. SEE "INVESTMENT REQUIREMENTS" AND "RISK FACTORS."

THE PARTNERSHIP IS SUBJECT TO SUBSTANTIAL CHARGES REGARDLESS OF WHETHER PROFITS ARE EARNED. SEE "DESCRIPTION OF CHARGES TO THE PARTNERSHIP."

THE PARTNERSHIP IS SUBJECT TO CONFLICTS OF INTEREST. SEE "CONFLICTS OF INTEREST AND RESPONSIBILITY OF THE GENERAL PARTNER."

THESE SECURITIES HAVE NOT BEEN APPROVED OR DISAPPROVED BY THE SECURITIES AND EXCHANGE COMMISSION NOR HAS THE COMMISSION PASSED UPON THE ACCURACY OR ADEQUACY OF THIS PROSPECTUS. ANY REPRESENTATION TO THE CONTRARY IS A CRIMINAL OFFENSE.

THE COMMODITY FUTURES TRADING COMMISSION HAS NOT REVIEWED THIS PROSPECTUS AND HAS NOT DETERMINED WHETHER IT IS ACCURATE OR COMPLETE.

	Price to Public	Selling Commissions (1) (2)	Proceeds to the Partnership (2) (3)
Per Unit (Minimum: 5 Units)	$ 1,000	(3)	$ 1,000
Total Minimum	$2,000,000	(3)	$2,000,000
Total Maximum	$5,000,000	(3)	$5,000,000

(Notes are on Page 2.)

CONTISECURITIES, INC.   **WHEAT, FIRST SECURITIES, INC.**

The date of this Prospectus is April   , 1979.

Any commodity futures fund must be accompanied by a prospectus giving specific information about managers, investment strategies, and past performance. This front page is from a prospectus prepared for a fund sponsored by ContiCommodity Services Inc.

lead to large losses as well as gains. Such trading losses
can sharply reduce the Net Asset Value of the partnership and consequently the value of your interest in the
partnership.

Under certain market conditions, the partnership
may find it difficult or impossible to liquidate a position. This can occur, for example, when the market
makes a "limit move." Placing contingent orders, such
as "stop-loss" or "stop-limit" orders, will not necessarily
limit the partnership's losses to the intended amounts,
since market conditions may make it impossible to
execute such orders.

This brief statement cannot, of course, disclose all
the risks and other significant aspects of investing in
the partnership. You should therefore study this Prospectus and commodity trading before you decide to
invest in the partnership.

Enough said. The game is tricky. Moreover, the investor
choosing to move into a pool also should be aware of the
management fees and commissions that he will have to
pay and the fact that, in most cases, it also costs him
money to redeem his shares in the pool. Yet, many of the
pools have proven to be very popular over the past few
years because they have been able to turn in good gains,
and as a result have produced hefty profits for many small
investors.

The majority of the pools rely on technical analysis and,
therefore, fund managers making investment decisions
generally are reacting to what a computer tells them to do.
But even the computers are not infallible. In 1975, for
example, Heinold Commodities Inc. of Chicago started up
a computerized fund with an initial nest egg of $6.3 mil-
lion. In the first quarter of 1976, the fund lost $5.5 million
of that total. Yet during that period it collected commissions of $2.5 million.

Again, as with opening up any type of account, make
sure you know with whom you are doing business. A list
of firms offering pools can be found in the final chapter.

WHAT ARE MANAGED ACCOUNTS?

Besides opening futures accounts in individual, joint, or

TRADING AUTHORIZATION LIMITED TO PURCHASES AND SALES OF COMMODITIES

Clayton Brokerage Co. of St. Louis, Inc.
7701 Forsyth, Suite 300
Clayton, Missouri 63105

Gentlemen:

The undersigned, _____

hereby authorizes _____
as his/her agent and attorney in fact to buy, sell (including short sales) and trade in
commodities and/or contracts relating to the same on margin or otherwise in accordance
with your terms and conditions for the undersigned's account and risk and in the
undersigned's name, or number, on your books. The undersigned hereby agrees to
indemnify and hold you harmless from and to pay you promptly on demand any and all
losses arising therefrom or debit balances due thereon.

In all such purchases, sales or trades, you are authorized to follow the instructions of the
above mentioned party in every respect concerning the undersigned's account with
you; and said party is authorized to act for the undersigned and in the undersigned's
behalf in the same manner and with the same force and effect as the undersigned
might or could do with respect to such purchases, sales or trades as well as with respect
to all other things necessary or incidental to the furtherance or conduct of such purchases,
sales or trades.

The undersigned hereby ratifies and confirms any and all transactions with you heretofore
of hereafter made by the aforesaid agent for the undersigned account.

This authorization and indemnity is in addition to (and in no way limits or restricts) any
rights which you may have under any other agreement or agreements between the
undersigned and your firm.

This authorization and indemnity shall be revoked automatically one year from the date
shown below, but until such time it shall be a continuing one and shall remain in full
force and effect until revoked by the undersigned by a written notice addressed to you
and delivered to your office at the above address, or by your firm by written notice to the
undersigned, but such revocation shall not affect any liability in any way resulting from
transactions initiated prior to such revocation.

_____
            (Date)

_____
   (City)   ·   (State)

_____   _____
            (Witness)   SIGNATURE OF CUSTOMER

SIGNATURE OF AUTHORIZED AGENT:

_____

*In setting up a managed account, an investor would have to sign
an agreement like this—used by Clayton Brokerage Co. of St.
Louis—granting power of attorney to another person.*

Clayton Brokerage Co. of St. Louis, Inc.
7701 Forsyth, Suite 300
Clayton, Missouri 63105

Gentlemen:

I have carefully examined the provisions of the document
by which I have given trading authority or control over my
account to:

_____
        (Name)   (Address)

and fully understand the obligations I have assumed by
executing that document.

I understand that your firm is in no way responsible for any
loss to me occasioned by the actions of the individual or
organization named above and that your firm does not, by
implication or otherwise, endorse the operating methods of
such individual or organization.

I further understand that neither the Chicago Board of
Trade, the Chicago Mercantile Exchange, the Kansas City
Board of Trade, the New York Mercantile Exchange, nor
any other commodity exchange on which orders may be
executed for my account, has any jurisdiction over a nonmember who is not employed by one of its members, and
that if I give to such individual or organization authority to
exercise any of my rights over my account, I do so at my
own risk.

                                        _____

_____
     (Date)

SPECIAL INFORMATION FORM FOR
CONTROLLED, MANAGED OR DISCRETIONARY ACCOUNTS

The rules of the Chicago Mercantile Exchange, pertaining to controlled, managed or discretionary accounts, require us to obtain certain facts concerning your financial resources and trading objectives. We therefore request your cooperation in completing the following form, to be held in strict confidence.

ACCOUNT NAME: _____

The following reasons best describe my goals with respect to my discretionary account:

Check appropriate items:

Short term capital gains   _____

Long term capital gains   _____

Other (Specify)   _____

My net worth is:

Under $25,000   ☐

$25,000 to $50,000   ☐

$50,000 to $100,000   ☐

Over $100,000   ☐

I understand that no funds other than risk capital are recommended to be used in commodity trading. I further understand that there are no guarantees as to profits in a managed, controlled or discretionary account program.

_____
Signature

_____
Date

company names—or joining a mutual fund—an individual trader can invest in the commodity markets by opening what is known as a managed account. Also referred to as discretionary or controlled accounts, managed accounts are structured in such a way that the trader signs over power of attorney to another person—usually his broker—who then has the authority to handle the person's account in any way he sees fit.

Of course, a situation like that raises quite a few questions about which actions or investments a manager may think are prudent and which that investor may think are prudent. As a result, the federal Commodity Futures Trading Commission (CFTC) and many of the various exchanges have established very strict guidelines as to what steps the manager may take in handling his customers' money. Moreover, the brokerage firms themselves have set up exacting rules under which the managers, especially if they also are the person's registered representative, must operate.

Among the regulations that the various exchanges have set up for managed accounts is one that requires that customers maintain a specific net equity position in their account—that is, a sum in excess of required margin for positions that still are open. At the world's largest futures market, the Chicago Board of Trade (CBOT), for example, net equity in managed accounts must total at least $5,000 more than required margins. If, at any time, the net equity position should fall below that level, exchange regulations require that the investor bring the position back up to that $5,000 level with additional deposits of money.

In addition, the CBOT also requires that managed accounts can be handled only by registered commodity representatives who have been with their respective firms for at least two years. And while those accounts may be managed by a junior person such as a registered representative, regulations generally also require that the junior person be supervised by an officer or a partner of the firm.

The safeguards are strict, for good reason. Consequently, managed accounts have proven to be quite popular with a number of investors over the past few years. A list of firms offering managed accounts can be found in the final chapter.

WHAT ABOUT COMMISSIONS?

One of the first things that a novice commodity futures trader must learn is the difference between commissions in futures trading and in stock trading. The most obvious difference is this: an investor in the stock market pays a commission both when he buys and when he sells. In the futures market, commissions are a one-time thing. Commissions are not paid when a trader opens a position. They only are paid when the position is closed.

Moreover, in stock trading, commissions can vary all over the lot depending on the number of shares bought or sold, the price of the shares, and the frequency with which the investor comes to market.

In commodities trading, however, commission rates are specified at a set rate per contract for each commodity. For example, to buy and then sell a soybean contract on the Chicago Board of Trade, an investor would have to pay his broker a commission of about $50.50. The commission on Treasury bond futures, however, would be somewhat steeper, about $61.

For active traders, commissions often can prove very costly over the course of a year. Therefore, in implementing trading strategies it is always important to factor in the cost of commissions to get an accurate measure of what your market position really is. Ask your broker for a complete commission schedule before you start trading, so that you will have extra information to consider when you are deciding in which commodity contracts to invest. A sample commission schedule is in the final chapter.

WHAT ABOUT DISCOUNT BROKERS?

While most investors are familiar with the fact that discount brokers have grown by leaps and bounds in the equities industry since fixed commission fees were freed on May 1, 1975, very few investors realize that discount brokers are beginning to flourish as well in the commodities futures industry.

That birth of discounters was the result of a decision in late 1974 by Northern Illinois Federal District Judge William Bauer. And those investors who need only execution capability from their brokerage houses—that is, those sophisticated investors capable of making their own investment decisions—have been the beneficiaries, for they have been able to pay only for the brokerage house services they really wanted.

One of the most important things to remember for prospective futures investors, however, is that it is not worth saving a few dollars in commissions if the investor does not feel qualified to make his own decisions. A good rule of thumb: If you have to worry about the costs of commissions you probably do not belong in the futures market in the first place. Discount brokers are for savvy investors who can afford, because of their own expertise, to do without the traditional firms' investment advice.

WHAT ABOUT MARGINS?

Like commissions, margins also are quite different in the futures market from what they are in the stock market.

Simply put, in stock trading the margin is used as a down payment (or part of the payment) for a specific amount of stock. Currently, margins are set at 50 percent. Therefore, an investor buying 1,000 shares of a $10 stock could purchase those securities with a margin payment of $5,000 and finance the remaining $5,000 through a loan from his broker. (Of course, interest would be charged on that loan.)

Commodity margins, meanwhile, are quite different. In commodities trading, initial margins are simply good-faith deposits that an investor gives his broker to verify his intention in the specific transaction.

Moreover, margins are much smaller in futures trading than in stock trading. To purchase a $1 million contract of U.S. Treasury bills on the Chicago Mercantile Exchange, for example, the initial margin required would be just $800, which contrasts sharply with the $500,000 margin that would be needed for a similarly sized transaction in stocks.

Because of these small margins, then, only the smallest of price moves can result in an investor doubling or even tripling his money. This "leverage" factor is probably the most appealing aspect of futures trading. But the leverage factor also works against the trader when the market goes against him, because of the maintenance margin.

Maintenance Margins

In the Treasury bill example above, the $800 initial margin is equal to 32 basis points per contract, and therefore would protect the brokerage house and the investor against a 32-basis-point change in the price of T-bills. If the investor bought a contract at a price of 90.32 in the expectation that quotes would rise, the position would be protected by the margin to a decline to 90. By the same token, if the trader had gone short, or invested on the belief that prices would decline, the price could rise to 90.64 before the margin protection was erased.

But the broker will not let this complete "wipe-out" occur, and when prices have moved against a trader's position significantly he will call for additional deposit funds known as maintenance-margin payments.

For example, in the T-bill case, the trader would be permitted to lose 25 percent of his initial margin, or $200, but would be required to "maintain" an equity position of 75 percent of the initial margin at all times. Therefore, a trader could expect a call from his broker if prices move adversely to his position. In the T-bill case, then, the long trader could stand a decline in price of 8 basis points, to 90.24, before he would be asked to provide additional margin payments.

In sum, the small margin requirements needed in the futures markets provide glorious opportunities for profit. But a warning: Your price forecasts still must be right. If prices go against you, your margin costs may well end up being steeper than you had planned.

The experiences of my good friend George the Greedy are nearly as valuable as the musings of Freddie the Lip.

George has always done very well in the stock market by being aggressive and by being a big spender. When he found a stock that interested him, he almost always took very large positions, up to $100,000 in some cases, figuring that only a modest advance in the price of the stock would translate into a quick 10 percent or 15 percent profit in a matter of days. And, to George's credit, he was right far more often than he was wrong.

But then George discovered the futures market, and its small margin requirements, and he began to salivate. The first time around, he had about $70,000 available to invest, and he did just that, placing the whole wad on initial margin payments for coffee futures. A week later, prices had declined to the point where George received a call from his broker saying that maintenance margin payments were necessary. His total available cash was tied up in the initial margins, but George didn't want to close out all of his positions because he felt that prices still were likely to rise. As a result, he chose the only alternative: he had to sell off some of his stocks at a loss to recoup enough money to pay the *maintenance* margins.

The moral of story: Anticipate the worst and be surprised by the best.

A list of sample initial and maintenance margins can be found in the final chapter.

MONITORING THE MARKET

To keep abreast of price changes in the futures market, a trader simply has to call his broker during the course of a day to get an update. In addition, many brokerage houses, as well as many of the futures exchanges, maintain market information hot lines which can be called to ascertain current prices. Check with your broker or an exchange's public-affairs department to find out what services they have available.

Also, quotes are printed daily in many newspapers— *The Wall Street Journal, The New York Times* and *The Chicago Tribune*, for example—and should be followed closely by investors.

While the tables in the different newspapers may vary in the way they present their information, the following table on p. 67 should give you a good idea of how to read the newspaper tables.

At the top of each grouping of prices is the specific commodity in question, the size of the contract, and the price in which that contract is quoted. For example, in the first case above, the quotes are for wheat, which is traded

Chicago Bd. of Trade

	High	Low	Settle close	Net chge.	Season's range High	Season's range Low
Wheat [5,000 bu.] dollars per bu.						
Dec	2.57	2.55	2.55½		3.47	2.24¾
Mar	2.65¾	2.62¾	2.65¼	+.00½	3.29	2.34
May	2.70	2.67	2.69½	+.00¾	3.20¾	2.38¾
Jul	2.73¾	2.71	2.73¼		2.99	2.46½
Sep	2.78¾	2.77	2.78½		3.03	2.48½
Dec	2.85¾	2.84¼	2.85½		3.11	2.78½
Corn [5,000 bu.]—dollars per bu.						
Dec	2.19	2.17	2.18½	+.01½	2.78¾	1.90
Mar	2.23¾	2.21⅞	2.23½	+.00¼	2.83¾	1.98¼
May	2.25¾	2.24	2.25½	+.00¼	2.86¾	2.06¾
Jul	2.26½	2.24¾	2.26¼	+00.½	2.72	2.06¾
Sep	2.23½	2.21¾	2.22¾	+.00½	2.37¾	2.09½
Dec	2.24¼	2.22¼	2.23½	+.00½	2.37½	2.20½
Oats [5,000 bu.] dollars per bu.						
Dec	1.31	1.30	1.30¼	—.00¼	1.73	1.07
Mar	1.35½	1.34	1.34¾		1.72	1.12¼
May	1.36	1.30	1.30¼	—.00¼	1.46	1.15
Jul	1.36½	1.35¾	1.36¼		1.45	1.15
Sep	1.36½	1.36½	1.36½	—.00¼	1.44¾	1.31
Soybeans [5,000 bu.] dollars per bu.						
Jan	6.01	5.88½	5.95½	+.03	7.99	5.04½
Mar	6.08	5.96½	6.03½	+.03¼	8.04½	5.13
May	6.14	6.02	6.10½	+.05	8.07½	5.20
Jul	6.18	6.07½	6.13¾	+.03¼	8.07	5.26½
Aug	6.13	6.05½	6.12	+.04	6.52	5.29¼
Sep	5.97½	5.92	5.95	+.00½	6.31½	5.23
Nov	5.96	5.87½	5.92	+.00½	6.25½	5.35
Jan	5.98	5.94	5.97½		6.20½	5.84½
Soybean Oil [60,000 lbs] dollars per 100 lbs.						
Dec	22.55	21.60	21.75	—.47	29.18	17.35
Jan	22.25	21.15	21.38	—.57	28.78	17.50
Mar	22.20	20.72	21.05	—.67	28 65	17.75
May	21.95	20.48	20.80	—.68	28.35	18.00
Jul	21.70	20.35	20.60	—.75	28.15	18.13
Aug	21 50	20.40	20.45	—.75	21.75	18.13
Sep	20.30	20.20	20.25	—.60	29.10	18.13
Oct	20.10	19.90	19.90	—.52	20.86	18.40
Soybean Meal [100 tons] dollars per ton						
Dec	163.00	161.50	162.90	+3 60	212.50	134.30
Jan	166.00	160.50	162.20	+2.90	212.00	136.50
Mar	166.00	161.50	164.20	+3.00	214.50	140.00
May	166.50	164 00	165.80	+2.50	216.50	143.50
Jul	168.50	167.00	168.30	+2.00	218.50	147.00
Aug	169.50	168.00	169.00	+1.00	181.00	148.00
Sep	167.00	165.00	166.00	+ 80	180.50	149.50
Oct	166.00	162.50	166.00	+2.00	178.50	150.50
Iced Broilers [30,000 lbs.] dollars per 100 lbs.						
Dec	36.60	36.35	36.35	+ .20	38.20	35 25
Jan	37.60	37.42	37.42	— .13	38.20	36.90
Feb	38.35	38.20	38.20	— .17	38.75	37 10
Mar			38.52		38.95	37.20
Apr	38.50	38.45	38.45	+ .15	38.75	38.05
May	38.70	36.65	38.70	+ .10	38.80	38.55
SILVER [5,000 troy oz.] cents per troy oz.						
Dec	466.50	462.90	463.30	—3.20	555.50	436.00
Jan	465.00	465.00	465.00	—1.50	496.00	465.00
Feb	471.80	466.00	466.80	—3.30	525.00	441.00
Apr	478 00	472 00	472.70	—3.30	531.00	447.60
Jne	484.50	479.00	479.30	—2.90	536.50	454.00
Aug	490.60	485.50	485.50	—2.50	560.00	459.50
Oct	496.70	491.80	491.80	—2.70	534.00	465.00
Dec	503.00	498 10	498.10	—2.90	538.00	471.00
Feb	509.50	503.00	504.30	—2.70	543.00	475.50
Apr	516.00	520 70	510.70	—2.80	550.00	493.50
Jne	522.40	517.10	517.10	—2.80	556.00	499.00
Aug	529.00	523.50	523 50	—3.00	563.00	504.50
Oct	535.50	529.90	529.90	—3 40	569.00	527.00
Dec	542.00	536.30	536.30	—3.20	575.40	534.00
Plywood [76,033 sq. ft.] dollars per 1,000 sq. ft.						
Jan	215.50	211.00	215.00	+5.00	219.40	162 00
Mar	218.00	213.00	215.80	+3.20	219.00	185.50
May	217.50	215.00	215.70	+2.50	217.80	190.00
Jly	217.30	215.50	215.80	+2.30	218.00	189.70
Sep	216.50	215.00	215.00	+1.50	217.30	189.00
Nov	215.00	213.00	213.00	+ .50	215.50	195.00
Jan	214.50	212.30	214.00	+1.50	214.80	208.00
GNMA—Pts and 32nds of 100 pct.						
Dec	97-00	96-24	96-25	—08	80-06	92-01
Mar	96-13	96-04	96-04	—10	98-16	92-28
Jne	95-29	95-21	95-21	—10	97-30	92-12
Sep	95-18	95-11	95-11	—10	97-16	91-26
Dec	95-09	95-02	95-02	—10	97-03	92-02
Mar	95-02	94-26	94-26	— 11	96-27	91-31
Jne	94-27	94-18	94-19	—10	96-30	93-09
Sep	94-20	94-14	94-14	—10	96-12	94-14
Dec	94-14	94-09	94-08	—10	96-01	94-08
Mar	94-05	94-01	94-01	—10	95-21	94-01
TREASURY BONDS—Pts and 32nds of 100 pct.						
Dec	100-18	100-08	100-08	—13	113-23	100-08
Mar	100-05	99-26	99-26	—15	103-08	99-26
Jne	99-25	99-15	99-15	—16	102-24	99-15
Sep	99-17	99-08	99-08	—14	102-14	99-08
Dec	99-03	99-02	99-02	—14	102-00	99-02
Mar	99-05	98-26	98-26	—16	101-26	99-06
COMMERCIAL PAPER [$1 Million]						
Dec			6.67	+ .02	7.12	6.30
Mar	7.10	7 08	7 08	— .04	7.43	6.76
Jne	7.56	7.52	7.56	+ .05	7.72	7.20
Sep	7.86	7.83	7.86	+ .02	7.95	7.55
Dec	8.06	8 03	8 06	+ .03	8.15	7.75
Mar	8.25	8.23	8.25	+ .02	8.48	8.00

in contracts of 5,000 bushels each and which is priced in dollars per bushel.

Along the left-hand side are the delivery months for the various contracts trading at that specific time; the nearest-term month is listed first. The "high" above the first column signifies the highest price of that day and the "low" stands for the lowest.

The "settle-close" refers either to the closing price reached that session or to the settlement price, which is determined by the exchange's clearing operation if the actual close happens to be a range of prices. The net change refers to the change from the previous day's close and the season's high and low signify the range in which that particular contract has traded.

THE EXCHANGE FLOOR

In all the various financial marketplaces that exist in the world, there surely is no sight that rivals the trading floor of a commodities futures exchange.

In an age where most stock exchanges are heatedly debating the relative merits of switching over to a higher degree of electronic and computer trading—and thus probably removing the human element from the trading floor—commodity exchanges are standing pat with their historical "open-outcry" auction system which effectively leaves trading to the individuals on the floor.

And because those individuals are on the floor, the floor of a futures exchange more often than not resembles an angry crowd on a street. All trading is done face to face between traders, confirmations are simply the pointing of a finger, and record keeping, for the most part, is based on a slip of paper that traders drop on the floor. It is a sight that has to be seen to be believed.

The trading floor is divided up into rings, or pits, each of which is the only place on the floor in which a specific commodity may be traded. For example, soybeans only can be traded in the soybean pit, wheat in the wheat pit, and so on.

In carrying out trades, the traders use hand signals to specify both price levels and their intentions either to buy or sell. For example, a raised hand, palm facing away,

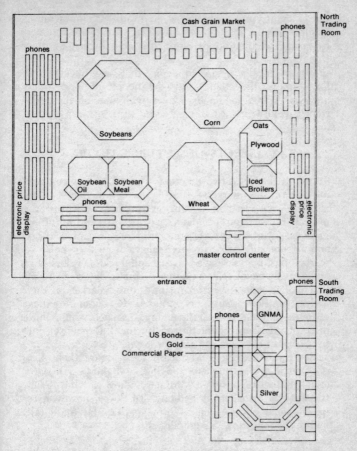

The trading floor of the Chicago Board of Trade is divided up into several trading pits, which are the only spots those contracts may be traded. (Diagram by Chicago Board of Trade)

would signify that the trader wanted to sell. Palm facing in would state the intention to buy. Price levels are signified by certain configurations of the fist and fingers, as illustrated on p. 71.

When a trader begins to signify that he wishes to sell, for example, the other traders in the pit respond to his motions. When he finally agrees with one of them the trade is complete.

TAX ASPECTS OF FUTURES TRADING

Just as there are two different types of traders comprising the futures markets—speculators and hedgers—there also are two ways of looking at the tax aspects of the market. Indeed, for speculators participating in the futures markets, futures contracts are considered as capital assets, and as such any profit or loss realized from a speculator's market position is viewed as a capital gain or loss. For hedgers, however, the situation is quite different. Firms that realize gains or losses in the futures market on their hedge positions must be required to factor in those changes in their cost of inventory. As such, then, those price changes are characterized by the Internal Revenue Service as either ordinary gains or losses.

For those taxpayers who wish to structure their positions so that they too are hedging, and thus arrange for any loss to be considered ordinary, they can have their transactions classified as hedging. To do so, however, requires some effort, such as proving that the trade falls within the following IRS guidelines:

· The investor faces a risk of loss by unfavorable changes in the price of a commodity expected to be used or marketed by one's businesses.
· The investor could shift such risk to someone else through the purchase or sale of futures contracts.
· The investor intends to attempt to shift that risk.

Another important factor that prospective futures players should consider is the process under which capital gains or losses are considered either long term or short term. Indeed, the calculation involves several elements.

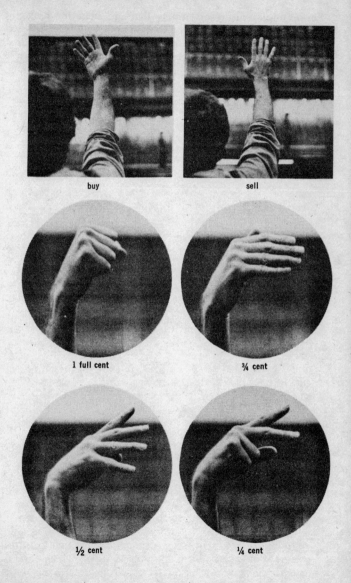

buy

sell

1 full cent

¾ cent

½ cent

¼ cent

For example, futures contracts that are held for longer than six months qualify to be treated on a long-term basis. But, because of the interesting straddle opportunities for tax reasons that futures present, it is always better to check with an accountant or lawyer to be sure of exactly what your liabilities may be.

IV. The Futures Market: How and Why Contracts Are Traded

Now that you have familiarized yourself with both the personalities of the commodity futures market and its basic fundamentals, it is time to develop a broader understanding of the "how" and the "why" of the fastest-growing investment game in America. It is imperative to understand the exact function of speculators and hedgers in the futures market, because without first understanding that the futures market is a financial marketplace with two distinct sides, a novice investor would simply be throwing away his money.

Moreover, the research efforts that go into developing commodity futures trading strategies also are far different from those used in the traditional stock and bond markets and therefore most American investors are not familiar with them. Consequently, it also is extremely important that any investor who has decided to declare war on inflation and attempt to fight back through the use of futures become familiar with the various analysis techniques used in this market.

WHAT IS A HEDGER?

In the commodity futures markets there are only two types of traders: the speculators and the hedgers. If you, as an individual, are thinking about investing in commodity futures, you are, quite simply, thinking about speculating. However, just as with any other type of transaction —whether it deals with stocks, bonds, or even obtaining loans from your bank—there has to be an entity on the opposite side of the transaction to make it work.

While public investors like you become speculators, commercial investors such as farmers, producers, warehousers, processors, and manufacturers become hedgers. They are investors who take positions in the futures markets to protect themselves against price changes that may occur in the spot commodity markets and sharply disrupt their operations. Hedging enables the commercial interests such as giant cereal producer General Mills Inc. to minimize its losses or maximize its profits by taking a position in the futures market opposite to its position in the spot, or cash, market.

If these commercial interests were not to utilize the hedging, or protective, techniques of the futures market, they surely would be speculating in the cash market—that is, risking their capital on the expectation that spot prices would not move adversely to their needs.

But most of these commercial interests realize the limitations and the vagaries of our economic system, and instead are increasingly choosing to "buy some price insurance." In doing so, they can pick from two types of hedging techniques: the short, or selling, hedge; and the long, or buying, hedge. The selling hedge would be used by the producer or an owner of a commodity, such as a wheat farmer, to insure the price at which he will ultimately sell the crop. The buying hedge would be used by a merchandizer or processor, such as General Mills, to lock in the cost that it will have to pay for the product.

For example, if General Mills needs to buy grain in six months to produce the cereals that it makes, the firm would be said to be short the cash product. To protect against price rises that may evolve in the spot market in those six months, the firm would employ the buying hedge and purchase a contract on a futures exchange for future delivery of exactly the amount of wheat that it will buy in the spot market on that date. By doing so, the company has eliminated any risks involved with price rises in the spot market that may occur by the time it needs the grain.

If prices do rise in the spot market, grain futures prices also will rise. Because General Mills bought the futures contract at a lower price, it will profit on the futures contract by an amount equal to the rise in the price of grain in the spot market. The firm, thus, will break even.

Similarly, a farmer in Kansas may employ a selling hedge to receive the same protection. If the farmer's crop will be ready for harvest in three months, he naturally is concerned about what prices in the spot market will be at that time. To protect himself, the farmer will "short the market" by selling futures contracts that promise to deliver an amount of wheat equal to that which he will harvest. If the cash price for wheat declines between the time he takes the position and the time his contract comes due, he is adequately protected by the hedge. By selling the contract to deliver three months earlier, the farmer has locked in the higher price that was prevailing at that time, which will compensate for the drop in prices that has occurred in the cash market.

Hedging techniques work because cash prices and futures prices have a tendency to move in tandem, provided supply-and-demand situations remain fairly stable. Indeed, both cash and futures prices are influenced by the same factors—supply and demand—and can be expected to respond similarly to a given set of circumstances. Chances are much higher that the difference between the two prices will remain stable than that prices in either the spot or the futures market will remain steady.

In the parlance of the futures markets, the difference between spot and futures prices is referred to as the "basis" and is expressed simply, in arithmetic terms. For example, if wheat is selling in the spot market in June for $4.39 a bushel, and the price of the July wheat futures contract on the Chicago Board of Trade is $4.43 a bushel, the basis would be expressed as "four cents under the July." (Of course, that would only be true in relation to the CBOT, and could vary with other exchanges that trade wheat futures.)

Moreover, the basis either could be stated as a positive or a negative number, though futures prices more often than not are higher than the spot prices. If the spot price is significantly below that in the futures market, it would be referred to as a "weak basis" and would indicate either low demand for the product or oversupply conditions. Conversely, a "narrow basis"—where the difference is small or even the case where the spot price is higher than the futures price—would indicate that the product is in short supply or that demand is high.

The basis illustrates several things, among them the cost of transportation between the locations of the cash commodity and the futures market, the difference in supply-and-demand conditions relative to the futures market and to where the cash commodities are located, and the variations in quality between the cash commodity and that specified in exchange contracts. Yet, as the futures contract approaches its expiration date, the basis tends to disappear because, theoretically, the supply-and-demand situations in both the cash and futures market start to become identical.

WHAT IS A SPECULATOR?

While the futures markets offer the commercial investors a unique opportunity to hedge their spot commodity operations, the futures markets would not exist if it were not for the individual investors: the speculators. Indeed, the futures market speculator plays a highly significant role because it is he who permits the hedger to transfer all of the risk of doing business onto the speculator's shoulders. But while in the majority of cases the hedger looks to transfer the risk of price fluctuations to assure that he will break even, the psychology of the speculator is far different.

Quite simply, in exchange for accepting the production and marketing risks that the commercial firm does not want, the speculator hopes that his riskier market position can be parlayed into a sweet profit.

Moreover, the speculator, whether a small individual investor or a large commodity mutual fund, is providing the futures market with two invaluable services: the infusion of capital and the building of a liquid market. Without this ongoing injection of funds, the futures markets would work neither for the speculators nor the hedgers. Indeed, to many market proponents, the activities of the speculators enable the commercial firms to have a much steadier handle on their costs—production, transportation, etc.—which in turn can result in smaller and fewer price increases being passed on from producers to consumers.

To be sure, in many ways the futures market speculator is the conduit between producers of commodities who want to make a profit and consumers of it who are usually trying to make do on a stringent budget. And the speculators by taking that middle position, in theory at least, are attempting to keep both sides happy.

Just as there are many types of hedgers in the futures game, so too are there many different types of speculators. Professional traders, securities firms, and members of the general public are all being increasingly drawn to the fast-paced futures markets because of the fantastic profit opportunities these markets offer for a relatively small initial investment.

This "leverage" is what sets the futures investment apart from other types. For example, generally speaking, an investor can take a position in the futures market for as small an initial investment as 5 percent to 15 percent of the total market value of the contract. By contrast, the current margin requirement on stock purchases is 50 percent.

To help differentiate, the jargon of the futures business has divided up the various types of speculating traders into several categories, such as:

• Day Trader: a speculator who is happy to make quick, small profits on the market. A day trader, like his name, usually holds market positions only during the course of a trading session, and seldom carries them over to the next day. This type of trading is regarded as the most difficult, because quick profits on short-term fluctuations can be very dangerous goals to accomplish.

• Position Trader: a participant who holds his position for much longer periods of time—days, weeks or months —because he has determined a long-term price forecast to which he is holding.

• Scalper: a speculator who is usually a professional trader, and like a day trader generally confines all his buying and selling to the current day. His attempt at large profits, then, is predicated on his high volume of trades. Moreover, a scalper, by virtue of his need to take numerous positions, often will buy and sell to complete transactions that others do not want.

• Spreader: a trader who acts similarly to an arbitrageur in that he attempts to profit from discrepancies in price relationships between two or more contracts, such as different delivery months for the same commodity, or those for the same month but which are traded on different exchanges.

Rules for Speculating

Because most futures speculators lose on the majority of their trades, it is important that the prospective commodities investor set up strict rules under which he will trade. Many so-called experts frequently tout their "systems," which they guarantee will result in a trader profiting a certain percentage of the time. The truth of the matter is this: If the system is so good that it always produces winners, the person or firm selling it to the public must be crazy to divulge such secrets. A good rule of thumb: STAY AWAY FROM ANYTHING THAT IS GUARANTEED.

But it is not necessary to stay away from speculating, despite the experiences of George the Greedy. And while questionable advice and help should be avoided like the plague, good advice from a reputable and respected firm or person should always be listened to and considered. With that in mind, the following "Suggestions to Sensible Speculation," as offered by ContiCommodity Services Inc., are worthy of note:

• LIMIT LOSSES, NOT PROFITS. This not only is the most important rule to remember in commodity speculation, but also the one most ignored. The professionals at Conti say that is because most American investors believe that price movements that go against their own predictions are merely "temporary aberrations" that will soon be corrected. The American investor, it seems, more times than not refuses to take a loss and admit a mistake. Yet the stop-loss orders available in the futures market give the investor just that opportunity.

At the same time, they say that too many futures investors close out positions when they have achieved small profits on the theory that "you can't lose money taking profits." Say the futures experts: "This rule has no place in commodity speculation. Experienced traders permit their profits to run until there is a clear indication of a change in market direction."

The bottom line is this: BY LETTING PROFITS RUN AND BY LIMITING LOSSES, THE FUTURES SPECULATOR HAS A BETTER CHANCE OF COMING OUT ON TOP. Why? Because it is proven that he will be wrong more times than right, and thus it is mandatory to achieve the largest possible profits on those few winning occasions to offset the more frequent, but usually much smaller, losses.

· DON'T TRADE ON RUMORS, TIPS, OR HUNCHES. Unlike investing in stocks, you are not likely to encounter a "hot" commodity that will climb in price without sound analytical reasons. A stock may increase because the company is going to come out with a new product that few people know about. That type of tip does not hold water in the futures market. Analysis is what is important in futures.

· TRADE WITH THE TRENDS, NOT AGAINST THEM. In any financial market there will be short-term technical reactions that go against a trend, but the safest bet is always to stay with the trend. The gamble you run in trying to time the length and magnitude of any technical reaction is much more difficult than spotting a long-term trend. Moreover, if you believe that prices will begin to trend upward within a short period of time, wait for that trend to actually manifest itself. The small amount of profit you may lose while waiting to be certain is well worth it.

· AVOID THE "ONE BASKET" TRADING APPROACH. The futures markets are risky enough without a trader increasing that risk ratio by limiting himself to just one commodity. Diversification is the way to succeed in futures. But be careful how you diversify. Three different positions in soybeans does not constitute a diversified portfolio because the soybean contracts, despite the fact that they might represent three different contract months, have a tendency to move up or down together. Spread your investing cash around.

· DON'T OVERTRADE. Don't feel guilty if you don't have

all your available investing capital sunk into the market. The smart trader knows when and how to invest. Success in futures trading is built on timing.

• LEARN HOW AND WHEN TO BUILD A POSITION. There are two major rules in this regard: (1) Don't add to a position until your most recently acquired contract shows a profit, and (2) additions to a profitable position should not be larger—in terms of number of contracts—than your original commitment. The first is especially interesting. After you first build a position, a subsequent price decline may lead you to think that an addition to that position, at the current lower price, is especially attractive. Actually, that lower price may not be telling you that it is an attractive buy, but that your original buy was not the correct move. The thing to do: Sit and wait until you have a better handle on what actually is happening.

• BE CAUTIOUS WITH "PAPER PROFITS." Too often a speculator thinks that his overall position is much healthier than it truly is because of the apparent profits he has "earned" on positions still open. As a result, the strict trading philosophies that he has adopted often are thrown to the wind as he gets greedier and greedier. Taking too aggressive or too large a position based on paper profits—which can disappear rapidly by a break in the market—is a very dangerous practice.

WHAT ARE THE FUNDAMENTAL AND TECHNICAL APPROACHES TO FUTURES ANALYSIS?

As in analyzing any type of prospective investment, there are several methods which may be used in attempting to evaluate the sometimes wild and woolly futures markets. But when it comes to analyzing the future direction of commodity prices, all methods basically are outgrowths of two main approaches: fundamental analysis and technical analysis. And while, at times, the two methods can become highly intricate, understanding them —and the principles on which they are based—is quite simple.

Indeed, the two methods clearly are what their names imply them to be. Fundamental analysis is a system which enables investors to predict price trends from studying the underlying factors that affect the supply and demand for the particular commodity on which the future is being traded. Perhaps the Chicago Board of Trade sums it up best in its *Commodity Trading Manual*: "The fundamental approach is based on the theory that the price of a commodity represents the equilibrium point at which the demand for a commodity and the supply of that commodity meet."

The technical approach is sharply different, however. An analysis of the market based on the technical approach would use current market activity, combined with historical performance of the market, to attempt to predict future movements.

While many futures market participants like to paint themselves as either fundamental or technical analysts, actually a great deal of analysis of commodity futures is based on a combination of the two disciplines. Indeed, any individual contemplating entry into the futures market would be foolish to limit himself to one certain type of analysis. The more work put into an investment decision, and the greater number of factors considered, often can spell the difference between success and failure. And success and failure in the futures markets is spelled d-o-l-l-a-r-s.

Fundamental Analysis

A fundamental analyst believes that he can construct a model that encompasses historical supply-and-demand factors for a certain commodity, as well as price movements during those historical periods, which will give him a clue as to how prevailing supply-and-demand considerations are likely to affect future prices. Notes the Chicago Board of Trade:

The steps involved in developing a model to forecast the price of a storable commodity might consist of:

1. gathering data indicating the components and levels of supply and demand for previous years.

2. comparing total supply and total demand to determine their net difference at the end of the year (the

year-end carryover) for each of these previous years.

    3. relating corresponding price levels to these historical total supply, total demand, and year-end carryover data.

    4. forecasting the next year's total supply, total demand, and resulting carryover, and

    5. using the forecast level of carryover and the historical relationship between prices and carryover to forecast future price levels.

The lengths an investor goes in developing his fundamental analysis can vary widely, depending on his experience in doing such analysis and the assistance he has in making his projections. Indeed, in recent years, the growing sophistication of computer systems has sharply enhanced the ability of fundamental analysts, who now occasionally use computers to help them factor emotional responses into their fundamental research.

Yet fundamental analysis does have some drawbacks. The primary one is that the information being fed into the model has been formulated by an individual and, therefore, in many cases is a subjective determination. But then again, if futures trading was merely the response of a human being to a flawless computer printout, the markets would not be as lively and volatile as they are nor would they present the interesting investment opportunities that they do.

Technical Analysis

"Fundamental analysis certainly has a place in choosing commodity futures investments. But, because of its limitations, for me, fundamental analysis really only is a complement to technical analysis." That comment, by a veteran of the futures game, is rather typical of a growing number of people in the industry who feel that technical analysis is a method of investment scrutiny far superior to fundamental analysis. While they agree that fundamental research has a value, they contend that its rigid parameters often result in predictions that cause investors to miss out on quick-hitting profit opportunities.

For example, says another futures official: "Fundamental analysis, based on historical patterns and forecasts for the upcoming year, may paint a picture of a relatively stable market for wheat over the next six months. On that basis, many traders might choose to ignore that commodity because of a lack of investment appeal. Yet technical analysis might indicate that the wheat markets should present several short-term profit opportunities during that same six-month period."

Indeed, the technician, or technical analyst, is looking more at the cracks that are hidden in the pricing structure of the market than just the entity as a whole, as would a fundamentalist. And the way that the technician would attempt to find those cracks is through the use of charts. To a technician, charts are as important a tool as a model is to the fundamentalist. By charting price behavior over long periods of time, a technician will look for patterns that are repeating themselves. And in the chartist's opinion, if events can be determined to have historical patterns, the chances are good that the same things will happen again.

My favorite technical analyst is Carmine the Computer, and he perhaps would be yours too if after meeting him, you were to listen to his views and watch him operate. Carmine always has been a whiz with computers. In college, so the story goes, he programmed the computer to tell him what time of day would be best to stage a protest rally and attract the largest crowd on campus. I wouldn't be surprised if the story is true because Carmine today still performs magic on the machines.

His hair is still long, though a little thinner, and his beard is still jet black, though a little thicker, than in his college days. But his expensive suits, spacious house, and two daughters give him away. Carmine is an enormously successful technician who does virtually everything he is instructed by his computers and charts. In September of every year, the computer says to buy a certain contract, and he does. In December it says sell, and he does.

Carmine is adamant in his belief that the computers will not let him down. On his winter vacations to Hawaii or Aspen, he is always accompanied by his wife, two children, and looseleaf binder of charts. His wife Kathy even jokes that the two children were conceived when the computer told Carmine the time was right.

There's an interesting sidelight to Carmine, however: He is forcing himself to use some fundamental analysis lately because he realizes that, despite his success, fundamental and technical analysis can complement each other very well. "I'm still a technician," he insists, "but I want to be a technician with a broad understanding of the markets."

THE ELEMENTS OF CHARTING

It is imperative that any investor new to the futures area fully educate himself to the intricacies of charting, that is, the types of charts that technicians prepare, and what to look for when studying those charts.

Basically, there are three types of charts which are used in commodity price forecasting: bar charts, moving-average charts, and point-and-figure charts. Each has a sharply different function and a full understanding of their purposes and limitations is essential to understanding the real futures markets. Discussions of the first two types follow (the point-and-figure chart is rarely used by novices), along with a look at other statistical material that technical analysts watch closely. In addition, a list of firms providing charting services can be found in the final chapter.

BAR CHARTS

Bar charts, probably the most popular and widely recognized type of charting technique, track price movements—daily highs, lows, and closes—for specific periods of time. For example, in the following chart of soybean prices provided by the Chicago Board of Trade the horizontal axis represents the passage of time (in this example the August-through-July period of 1964–1965) while the vertical axis signifies prices. The prices are plotted in the following way: The vertical lines span the day's high and low prices touched during the day's trading. The small cross line represents the day's closing price:

While keeping a bar chart up to date is relatively simple, reading the price information that such a tool is supposed to show to investors is somewhat more complicated. For example, the most basic information that a bar chart indicates to a market technician is the so-called support and

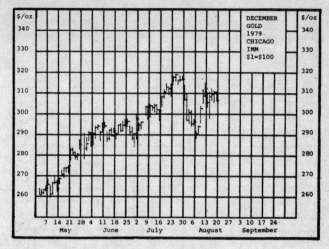

(Chart by Clayton Brokerage Co. of St. Louis)

resistance areas that appear in a contract's movement from one price level to another. Simply put, the support area can be described as the price level (which previously had been touched) that prices fall back to after posting a rally. The following chart illustrates two different support areas that manifested themselves during a prolonged market rally:

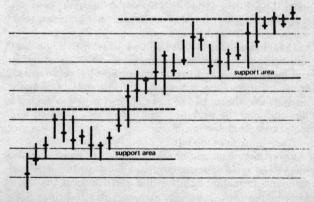

(Chart by the Chicago Board of Trade)

By the same token, the resistance area is a previously
touched price level that prices rally to before falling back.
The following chart illustrates two such resistance areas:

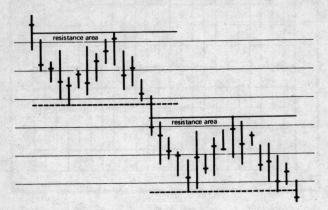

(*Chart by the Chicago Board of Trade*)

In addition to the support and resistance areas, bar
charts also vividly indicate market tops and market bottoms through the development of the so-called head-and-
shoulders, or inverted head-and-shoulders, patterns, which
follow:

Commodities market technicians believe that the head-
and-shoulders formation is a highly reliable indication that
the market is about to enter a significant reversal period.
Once the neck line is completed off the right shoulder,
analysts say, the degree of price change between the top of
the head and the neck line will be equaled in an opposite
move away from the neckline.

As can be discerned from the charts above, the head-
and-shoulders configuration signifies the end of a bull
market, or advancing market, and the inverted head-and-
shoulders formation indicates the end of a bear market, or
declining market.

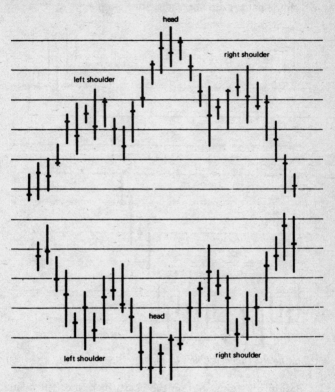

(Chart by the Chicago Board of Trade)

Another common configuration that technicians look for is a gap, which shows up on a chart as a price area in which the market did not trade. For example:

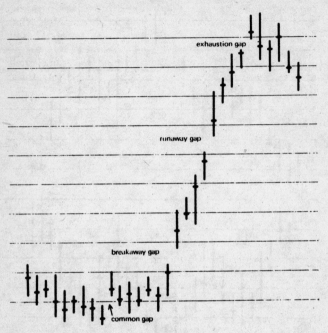

(Chart by the Chicago Board of Trade)

Basically, as indicated on the chart, there are four main types of gaps:

· **Common Gap:** can appear at any time and has no great significance.
· **Breakaway Gap:** follows a period of very narrow trading and may indicate a sharp movement in the future.
· **Runaway Gap:** occurs after a sharp breakaway has begun and may indicate the midway point of that movement.
· **Exhaustion Gap:** occurs after a lengthy and sharp movement in one direction and usually indicates a key reversal will follow.

MOVING-AVERAGE CHARTS

In addition to bar charts, a great number of market technicians also believe that moving-average charts are highly reliable at tracking and predicting market performance. That's because, they say, the irregularities that hamper daily charting techniques are smoothed out through use of the moving-average technique.

A moving-average chart can cover any time frame, such as three days, five days, or even thirty days. Using three days as the span, the plotting of such a chart follows:

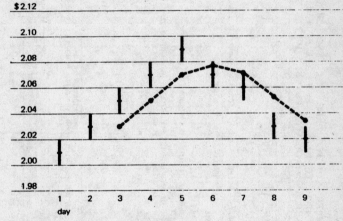

(Chart by the Chicago Board of Trade)

In the example above, day one represents the first three trading days, which resulted in closing prices of $2.00, $2.01, and $2.02, or an average of $2.01 as signified by the small cross line. Days four, five, and six, therefore, are averaged for day two on the chart and so on.

In reading and evaluating a moving-average chart, the technician is looking for the continuation of either an upward or downward trend. Any break in such a pattern, therefore, would likely be read as a break in the market and a signal to change market exposure.

VOLUME AND OPEN INTEREST

Many technicians also believe that analyzing the futures

LUMBER—CHICAGO MERCANTILE EXCHANGE
COMMITMENTS OF TRADERS IN ALL FUTURES
COMBINED AND INDICATED FUTURES, JULY 31, 1979

FUTURES	TOTAL OPEN INTEREST	REPORTING (LARGE) TRADERS								NONREPORTING TRADERS SPECULATIVE AND HEDGING (SEE EXPLANATORY NOTES)	
		SPECULATIVE				HEDGING		TOTAL			
		LONG OR SHORT ONLY		LONG OR SHORT (SPREADING)							
		LONG	SHORT	LONG	SHORT	LONG	SHORT	LONG	SHORT	LONG	SHORT
		(CONTRACTS OF 100,000 BOARD FEET)									
ALL	8,898	1,817	516	2,023	1,778	1,224	2,558	5,064	4,852	3,834	4,046
OLD	6,809	1,969	637	1,050	1,023	1,061	2,122	4,080	3,782	2,729	3,027
OTHER	2,089	360	300	461	334	163	436	984	1,070	1,105	1,019
		CHANGES IN COMMITMENTS FROM JUNE 30, 1979									
ALL	+1,518	−148	−391	−822	−667	−345	+947	−329	+1,223	−1,189	+295
		PERCENT OF OPEN INTEREST HELD BY EACH GROUP OF TRADERS									
ALL	100.0%	20.4	5.8	22.7	20.0	13.8	28.7	56.9	54.5	43.1	45.5
OLD	100.0%	28.9	9.4	15.4	15.0	15.6	31.2	59.9	55.5	40.1	44.5
OTHER	100.0%	17.2	14.4	22.1	16.0	7.8	20.9	47.1	51.2	52.9	48.8
	NUMBER OF REPORTING TRADERS										
ALL	50	23	11	22	22	10	12	44	37		
OLD	48	22	11	16	15	8	12	37	33		
OTHER	27	9	9	9	9	5	7	21	19		

CONCENTRATION RATIOS
PERCENT OF OPEN INTEREST HELD BY THE INDICATED NUMBER OF LARGEST REPORTING TRADERS

	BY GROSS POSITION				BY NET POSITION			
	4 OR LESS TRADERS		8 OR LESS TRADERS		4 OR LESS TRADERS		8 OR LESS TRADERS	
	LONG	SHORT	LONG	SHORT	LONG	SHORT	LONG	SHORT
ALL	17.9	22.7	26.8	32.2	10.0	15.4	15.2	19.2
OLD	19.5	25.8	29.9	37.1	12.8	18.2	19.7	23.0
OTHER	26.4	23.3	34.2	36.0	17.7	16.6	22.8	25.9

market's volume and open interest figures can be extremely helpful in predicting market behavior.

In other words, volume figures are a measure of the number of contracts traded in a specific commodity on any particular day. In analyzing volume figures, analysts generally believe that rising volume during a bull market means a continuation of price increases and that rising volume during a bear market signifies a continuation of price decreases. However, if volume should pick up substantially following a sharp price move, they believe that a major price reversal may be imminent.

Open interest, meanwhile, is the number of contracts on a specific commodity which have not yet been liquidated. According to the technicians, if open interest increases while prices also are rising, long hedgers or speculators (investors anticipating price increases) are entering the market and short hedgers or speculators (investors anticipating price decreases) are leaving. If this trend continues for several days, analysts feel the market is strong and likely for further advances.

If, however, open interest starts to decline despite a continued rise in prices, analysts generally believe that the market is weakening and that the traders with short positions are buying contracts back from the longs.

COMMITMENTS OF TRADERS

Another method technical analysts employ to follow the futures market is to study the Commitments of Traders manual that the Commodity Futures Trading Commission publishes each month.

Published the tenth day of each month and carrying statistics for the entire previous month, the booklet carries a breakdown of open interest figures for all commodity futures contracts. Specifically, the report documents the total long and short positions of large speculators, large hedgers, spreaders, and small speculators and hedgers.

The statistics are studied very closely by technical analysts, who look for unusual positions held by the large interests, which could indicate a changing view of how the market looks.

V. The Futures Market: Its Products and Exchanges

THE VARIOUS PRODUCTS

Not all futures contracts are appropriate for all investors. In much the same way that you should choose carefully before investing in a specific stock, the same exercise in caution should be used before spending your first dollar to assume a position in the futures market.

George the Greedy's next-door neighbor, Earl the Ear, didn't use caution and paid dearly. Earl is an extremely interesting person with a wide "glad-to-see-you" smile and a nice thing to say about everyone. He does have one glaring fault, however: Earl is a professional follower. If someone else does something, Earl feels that he should do it too.

And he does. And when it came to playing around with futures, Earl ended up with the short stick because he didn't take the time to consider that an investment that works well for someone else might not fit his specific needs.

One November day a few years back, Earl was riding home from work on his commuter train when the conversation from the seat immediately to the rear grabbed his attention. The two men—and Earl could only hear portions of the conversation—were discussing commodity futures and how well certain ones were working out. Earl immediately assumed that the two men were talking about an investment opportunity that would mean a big payoff.

The next day he bought a sizable chunk of contracts in the commodity they were discussing. A few weeks later he was nearly wiped out. Why? The two men had indeed been discussing commodity contracts that were working out well. However, by working out well, they meant that the specific commodity was undergoing significant declines in price to make their short positions very profitable. Earl, meanwhile, had thought the men had gone long, had never taken the time to research the commodity himself, and learned a very expensive lesson in futures trading.

Remember: You can never over-research an investment.

Following are brief descriptions of most of the contracts currently available, the exchanges on which they are traded, and some pointers on how to evaluate the markets. In addition, charts have been provided on some of the contracts to illustrate historic price movements and lists of periodic reports have also been included for each of the various groupings.

Grain Commodities

WHEAT

For many investors, especially those who have used the commodities markets for a number of years, wheat futures rank high on the list of favorites. Indeed, not only is wheat one of the most important agricultural products in the United States, but futures on that commodity are one of the oldest established contracts as well. For those reasons it is not surprising that wheat futures are traded on four major U.S. commodity exchanges: the Chicago Board of Trade, the Minneapolis Grain Exchange, the Kansas City Board of Trade, and the MidAmerica Commodity Exchange.

Moreover, wheat futures are a favorite of many investors because of the volatility that characterizes the market. And that has been especially true in the past few years, because of the increased number of wheat sales between the United States and such trading partners as Russia and China. Such sales, as well as the rumors of such sales, help to make wheat futures an investment with both high liquidity and high volatility. For an investor looking for those qualities, wheat futures are indeed a handy investment vehicle.

For example, in 1978 the prospects of a wheat crunch caused futures prices to rise sharply. On the Chicago Board of Trade prices rose to $3.68 a bushel from $2.69 a bushel during the course of the year, primarily because there was a shortage of Soft Red Winter Wheat, one of the various types of wheat on which contracts are based. Prices also were catapulted higher by reports during the year that farmers would be planting fewer acres of their land to wheat and by the inclement weather that affected many parts of the country.

Basically, there are two types of wheat grown in the United States on which futures are traded. The first crop of the year, known as Winter Wheat, is harvested between late May and late July. Hard Red Winter Wheat is the variation most grown and it is raised primarily in the Southwestern and Western states. Another type, Soft Red Winter Wheat, is grown largely in the Midwest. Spring Wheat, meanwhile, is harvested late in the summer and is grown in the Plains states.

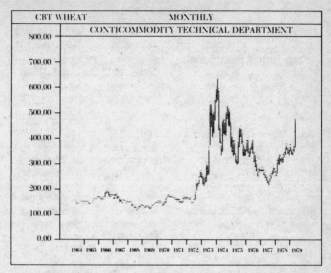

From 1964 to 1972 wheat futures prices were relatively stable in trading on the Chicago Board of Trade. Since that time, however, prices have been on a roller-coaster ride that has presented several profit opportunities. Price in cents per bushel. (Chart by ContiCommodity Services Inc.)

SOME OTHER FACTS ABOUT WHEAT: There are five contract months for wheat futures: March, May, July, September, and December. Other than the major classifications of wheat, there are a few more varieties, including Durum, which is grown in North Dakota and is used for such things as spaghetti and macaroni, and White Wheat, which is raised in New York State, Michigan, and the West Coast. The crop year for wheat in the U.S. runs from July 1 to June 30. Crop years are used in much the same way that corporations use fiscal years: to measure annual results in a way that is meaningful to the seasonality of a specific crop.

The Wheat Markets

Exchange	Size of Contract	Minimum Price Fluctuation	Daily Limit Price Fluctuations
Chicago Board of Trade	5,000 bushels	¼ cent per bushel or $12.50 per contract	20 cents a bushel ($1,000 per contract) compared with previous session's close
Kansas City Board of Trade	5,000 bushels	¼ cent per bushel or $12.50 per contract	25 cents a bushel ($1,250 per contract) compared with previous session's close
Minneapolis Grain Exchange	5,000 bushels	⅛ cent per bushel or $6.25 per contract	20 cents a bushel ($1,000 per contract) compared with previous session's close
MidAmerica Commodity Exchange	1,000 bushels	⅛ cent per bushel or $1.25 per contract	20 cents a bushel ($200 per contract) compared with previous session's close

CORN

While not as exciting a commodity as wheat, corn nevertheless has many avid followers in the futures markets, which makes it, like wheat, a highly liquid investment vehicle. In addition, as corn was unknown outside the Western world until Christopher Columbus decided to take some samples back to Europe after landing in America in 1492, corn has a uniqueness to it.

To be sure, those facts are not the only considerations weighed in declaring corn as the United States' most important crop. Indeed, farmers devote more of their land each year to the growing of corn, and the product regularly ranks number one in terms of the dollar value of the year's harvest.

Yet a very small portion, only about 20 percent, of the corn crop ever finds its way to the consumer. That part of the harvest is known as the cash corn crop, and is manifested in products for the consumer that actually are the vegetable or its derivatives, such as syrups and oils. The remaining portion of the production never leaves the farm, however, as it principally is used for feed and seeding purposes.

In large part it is this nation's ability to produce massive corn crops that has resulted in the corn futures market being rather dormant in the past few years. In fact, 1978 corn production was the largest ever in the United States. Combined with the hefty harvest of the previous year, it put a great deal of pressure on corn prices in 1978. Prices began at $2.19 a bushel in January, 1978, and rose above $2.50 in July before ending the year at around $2.30 a bushel.

SOME OTHER FACTS ABOUT CORN: There are between 100 and 150 different varieties of corn grown. The Corn Belt (Illinois, Indiana, Iowa, Minnesota, Missouri, Nebraska, Ohio, and South Dakota) is the principal producing region. Planting starts in early May, harvest in mid-October. The crop year runs from October 1 to September 30. The contract months for corn futures are March, May, July, September, and December.

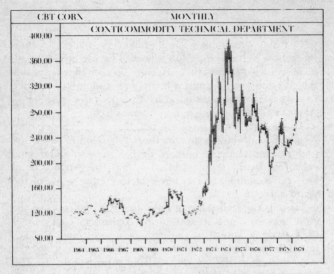

Like wheat futures, whose prices generally run in tandem with corn, corn futures have been especially volatile during the dynamic 1970s. Price in cents per bushel. (Chart by ContiCommodity Services Inc.)

The Corn Markets

Exchange	Size of Contract	Minimum Price Fluctuation	Daily Limit Price Fluctuations*
Chicago Board of Trade	5,000 bushels	¼ cent per bushel or $12.50 per contract	10 cents per bushel ($500 per contract) compared with previous session's close
MidAmerica Commodity Exchange	1,000 bushels	⅛ cent per bushel or $1.25 per contract	10 cents per bushel ($100 per contract) compared with previous session's close

  * Limit is raised to 150 percent of normal following three limit moves in succession.

OATS

Like corn, oats are a grain crop. And, in much the same way that only a small portion of this country's corn crop ever makes its way to the consumer's kitchen table, the same can be said about our oat output. Indeed, the Chicago Board of Trade says that only about 7 percent of the United States' total oat production is used for oatmeal and other cereal-type products by the American consumer. Another 8 percent is used for seeding. The rest, a whopping 85 percent or so, is used by farmers and ranchers for feeding their livestock, such as horses.

The similarities with corn do not end there, however, for oat futures prices generally follow the lead of the corn market and are fairly stable. Yet supply-and-demand considerations can clearly render that maxim useless. In 1978, for example, oat prices did not follow the lead set by corn, because the two commodities have sharply different supply characteristics.

In fact, the oat crop turned out to be sharply lower than many people had expected, and as a result, oat prices were stronger than had been forecast. Indeed, prices had declined to $1.24 a bushel in July from $1.32 in January before the lack of supply caused a resurgence that brought prices to $1.37 a bushel by year-end. In contrast, a record corn crop caused hefty price declines for corn in the same July-December period that proved to be strong for oats.

There are various classifications for oats, including Red Oats, White Oats, Black Oats, Gray Oats, and Mixed Oats. White Oats, however, are the type mainly grown and generally are found in Minnesota, North Dakota, and South Dakota. White Oats are planted in the early spring, and by late August the harvest usually is complete.

The seeding and harvesting schedules for the other varieties differ greatly, as oats are grown across the United States and thus encounter varying types of weather. However, the official crop year has been set at July 1 through June 30.

SOME OTHER FACTS ABOUT OATS: While oat production in this country has averaged less than one billion bushels annually for the past few years, production in the mid-1940s was sharply higher, regularly averaging about 1.5 billion bushels. The recent fall-off is because of a sharp

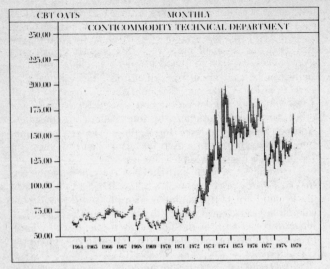

After rising sharply in the early 1970s, oat futures prices plunged markedly during 1977. They since have recouped most of that loss, however. Price in cents per bushel. (Chart by ContiCommodity Services Inc.)

The Oat Markets

Exchange	Size of Contract	Minimum Price Fluctuation	Daily Limit Price Fluctuations*
Chicago Board of Trade	5,000 bushels	¼ cent per bushel or $12.50 per contract	Six cents per bushel ($300 per contract) compared with previous session's close
MidAmerica Commodity Exchange	5,000 bushels	⅛ cent per bushel or $6.25 per contract	Six cents per bushel ($300 per contract) compared with previous session's close

* Limit is raised to 150 percent of normal following three limit moves in succession.

decline in the number of acres planted to the crop. Oat futures also are traded in Canada on the Winnipeg Grain Exchange. The contract months for oat futures in the United States are July, September, December, March, and May.

PERIODIC REPORTS ON GRAIN

U.S. Agricultural Marketing Service
  Feed Market News (weekly)
  Grain Market News (weekly)
  National Stock of Grain Report (weekly)
U.S. Bureau of the Census
  Current Industrial Reports, Flour Milling Products (monthly)
U.S. Crop Reporting Board
  Agricultural Prices (monthly and annually)
  Crop Production (monthly and annually)
  Grain Stocks (quarterly)
U.S. Economic Research Service
  Feed Situation (five per year)
  Wheat Situation (quarterly)
U.S. Foreign Agricultural Service
  Foreign Agriculture Circular, Grain (irregular intervals)
Commodity Futures Trading Commission
  Stock of Grain in Deliverable Positions (weekly)

Soybeans

THE SOYBEAN COMPLEX

Soybeans, which are the world's most popular source for edible high-protein meals, also are one of the world's oldest cultivated crops. It is known, for example, that soybeans were grown in China some five thousand years ago. Yet, until the early 1900s, there was very little soybean production outside of the Orient.

Large production of the crop began in the U.S. in the mid-1930s when it was discovered that soybeans had more value than just as a hay-forage crop with which to feed animals. Today, for example, soybean production in the United States accounts for nearly 75 percent of the total world consumption.

As important as the crop is, soybeans really have little value on their own. It is in the form of soybean meal and soybean oil that the demand for soybeans is rooted. For instance, soybean meal is produced as a light protein feed ingredient or for further processing into soy grits, flour, or isolated protein for use in food that will be consumed by humans. Soybean oil, meanwhile, is used in a variety of salad and cooking oils, margarine, and industrial chemicals.

The following table, prepared by the Chicago Board of Trade, shows the uses of the crop:

Whole Soybeans:
—crop seeding
—baked: soybeans and sprouts
—livestock feeds
—puffed soybeans
—steamed soybeans
—roasted soybeans
—full-fat soy flour
—soy butter
—soy cereal
Soybean Oil:
—refined soybean oils:
1. food uses: cooking, salad oil, margarine, mayonnaise, spreads, and prepared foods
2. industrial uses: adhesives, inks, plastics, and disinfectants
—soybean lecithin:
1. food uses: emulsifiers, coatings, and nutrients
2. industrial uses: antifoam agents, dispensing agents, stabilizing agents, and antiknock additives

—sterols
—fatty acids
—glycerols
Soybean Meal:
—feed uses: livestock feeds, poultry feeds, and pet foods
—industrial uses: fertilizers and fillers
—soy flour and grits:
1. food uses: bakery confections, cereals, beverages, soups, meat products, baby food, and dietetic foods
2. industrial uses: adhesives and coatings
—isolated proteins
—soybean millfeeds

Because soybeans are this country's third-largest crop, and because of their wide variety of uses (as noted above), investing in the crop's futures contracts can be inviting. The inflation that has haunted the U.S. during the 1970s has caused many investors to look for investments of a more speculative nature, and soybean futures have repeatedly been the choice of many.

During the course of 1978, for example, the prices for all three contracts, soybeans, meal and oil, rose sharply on futures exchanges. On the Chicago Board of Trade, soybeans climbed to $6.79 a bushel from $5.65 in January; oil increased to 25.82 cents a pound from 20.84; and meal climbed to $188.80 a ton from $162.20.

While inflation and standard soybean supply-and-demand considerations play a large role in determining the direction of soybean prices, the contracts also are affected by other factors. Although soybeans are classified scientifically as legumes, they nevertheless over the years have been more closely associated with the grains. As a result, when considering investments in any of the three sectors of the soybean complex, the futures market investor also should study other feed grains to understand the overall supply-and-demand picture.

The largest producing states for soybeans are: Illinois, Iowa, Indiana, Missouri, Minnesota, and Arkansas. Planting takes place in May or June and harvest usually occurs in September or October.

SOME OTHER FACTS ABOUT SOYBEANS: On the CBOT, the contract months for both meal and oil are January, March, May, July, August, September, October, and December. For soybeans they are January, March, May,

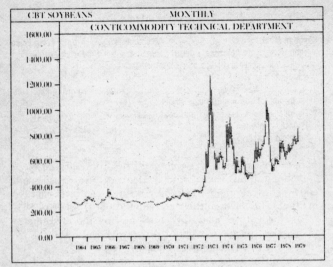

The bull market for soybean futures in 1973 was in sharp contrast to the sideways-moving market that prevailed during most of the 1960s. Price in cents per bushel. (Chart by ContiCommodity Services Inc.)

July, August, September, and November. On the Mid-America Commodity Exchange, the contract months for soybeans are January, March, May, July, August, and September.

The Soybean Markets

Exchange	Size of Contract	Minimum Price Fluctuation	Daily Limit Price Fluctuations*
Chicago Board of Trade			
(soybeans)	5,000 bushels	¼ cent per bushel or $12.50 per contract	30 cents a bushel ($1,500 a contract) compared with previous session's close
(oil)	60,000 pounds	1/100 cent per pound or $6 per contract	One cent per pound ($600 per contract) compared with previous session's close
(meal)	100 tons	10 cents per ton or $10 a contract	$10 a ton ($1,000 per contract) compared with previous session's close
MidAmerica Commodity Exchange			
(soybeans)	1,000 bushels	⅛ cent per bushel or $1.25 per contract	30 cents per bushel ($300 per contract) compared with previous session's close

* Limit is raised to 150 percent of normal following three limit moves in succession.

PERIODIC REPORTS ON SOYBEANS

U.S. Agricultural Marketing Service
  Feed Market News (weekly)
  Grain Market News (weekly)
U.S. Bureau of the Census
  Current Industrial Reports, Fats and Oil (monthly and
    annually)
U.S. Crop Reporting Board
  Crop Production (monthly and annually)
  Grain Stocks (quarterly)
  - Soybean Stocks (annually)
U.S. Economic Research Service
  Fats and Oils Situation (five per year)
  Feed Situation (five per year)
U.S. Foreign Agricultural Service
  Foreign Agricultural Circular, Oilseeds and Products (ir-
    regularly)

Forest Products

LUMBER AND PLYWOOD

Futures traded on forest products are some of the more attractive contracts available in the commodity markets. A variety of reasons account for that, not the least of which is the fact that their performance is closely related to a number of economic factors that affect the country, such as interest rate movements, the construction of residential housing, and the financial health of various industries. Indeed, in 1978 prices for both stud lumber and plywood, the two forest-product varieties on which futures contracts are traded, rose for the third year in succession despite predictions that higher interest rates would produce a sharp downturn in construction.

Though generally regarded as agricultural commodities, forest-product futures differ sharply from other "agricom-

Plywood futures prices rose sharply between December 1978 and early February 1979 before settling into a rather prolonged decline. Price in dollars per thousand square feet. (Chart by Clayton Brokerage Co. of St. Louis)

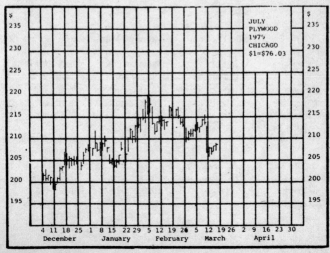

modities" in many ways and prospective investors in these
contracts should educate themselves fully on the differences. The most obvious is the amount of time needed to
grow and raise the product (many years) compared with
the much shorter span for other agricultural products.
Moreover, while almost all of the land on which other
agricultural commodities grow in the United States is
owned privately, about 28 percent of the nation's forest
lands are owned by the public. For example, according to
the Chicago Board of Trade, 12 percent of this land is
owned by the National Forests, 13 percent is owned by
forest product companies, and the rest by private companies and individuals.

Interestingly, many of the factors relating to the forest-
product futures market have changed greatly in recent
years. For example, through the early 1960s, nearly all of
the United States' plywood was produced from the
Douglas firs grown in this country's Pacific Northwest
region. That percentage now is down to about 80 percent,
however, caused by the growing use of pine emanating in
the southern United States.

SOME OTHER FACTS ABOUT LUMBER AND PLYWOOD: The
contract months for both stud lumber and plywood are
January, March, May, July, September, and November.

The Plywood and Lumber Markets

Exchange	Size of Contract	Minimum Price Fluctuation	Daily Limit Price Fluctuations
Chicago Mercantile Exchange (stud lumber)	100,000 board feet	10 cents per 1000 board feet or $10 a contract	$5 per 100 board feet ($5000 per contract) compared with previous session's close
Chicago Board of Trade (plywood)	76,032 square feet	10 cents per 1000 square feet or $7.6032 a contract	$7 per 1000 square feet ($532.224 per contract) compared with previous session's close

More than half the plywood and two-by-four stud lumber produced in this country is used in residential construction.

PERIODIC REPORTS ON FOREST PRODUCTS

U.S. Bureau of the Census
  Construction Reports:
    Housing Authorized by Building Permits (monthly and annually)
    Housing Starts (monthly)
    Value of New Construction Put in Place (monthly)
  Current Industrial Reports:
    Lumber Production and Mill Stocks (annually)
    Softwood Plywood (annually)
U.S. Forest Service
  Demand and Price Situation for Forest Products (annually)
  Production, Prices, Employment, and Trade in Northwest Forest Industries (quarterly)
American Plywood Association, Tacoma, Washington
  Plywood Statistics (weekly)
  Monthly Market Report (monthly)
C.C. Crow Publications, Portland, Oregon
  Crow's Weekly Letter (weekly)
  Crow's Weekly Plywood Letter (weekly)
Random Lengths, Eugene, Oregon
  Random Lengths (weekly)
  Random Lengths Export Market Report (biweekly)

Textiles

COTTON

The King.

For years, cotton has reigned as King of the Crops, both because of its importance to the country as a generator of revenue and also because of its volatile price movements in the futures markets, where it provided and took away many a fortune.

Just ask Delta Dave, my septuagenarian friend from the South. Dave, a kindly old Southern gentleman with a never-ending interest in investment, has experienced many bull and bear cotton markets through the years. And the college educations of his children have risen and fallen on those markets as well.

Son Bill was the first to feel the effects of the King. While a senior in high school, Dave was all prepared to go to night school upon graduation to continue his education because he knew the family did not have enough money to pay for his full-time education at a university. But Delta Dave had other ideas, especially when he heard through a friend that the heavy rain that year was going to spur a cotton shortage that was sure to drive up prices.

Dave immediately bought futures contracts in cotton and waited for his ship to come in. And it did, in large doses, after the federal government issued an announcement a few weeks later estimating that year's cotton crop at 19 percent smaller than had been anticipated. That September Bill started college full-time, and four years later he graduated with a degree in electrical engineering.

Six years later Dave ran into problems when he used the same technique to finance daughter Billie's education. While Delta cotton production was down, as he had anticipated, production elsewhere in the country was extremely heavy, more than making up for the shortage. Dave's long positions in the market were wiped out. Billie worked in a bank for a year, earning some money of her own, and she started school the following year.

While the cotton market is not the frenzied market-place it was in those years, because of the greater role the U.S. government has taken in the market, cotton futures still are a vehicle that can be very attractive to speculative investors.

World production of cotton generally has stayed around the 60-million-bale level for the past five years, with the United States, the Soviet Union, and mainland China the top three producers. In the United States four main areas of the country account for nearly all of our domestic production. For example, the Delta and the Southwest each account for about 33 percent of the output, according to the Chicago Board of Trade. Following on their heels are the West and Southeast, with 20 percent and 10 percent, respectively. The remainder is scattered across the country.

As Delta Dave could tell you, both cotton production and prices are very dependent on weather conditions as well as diseases carried by insects. Great amounts of production can be all but wiped out by either too little or too much rain, sun, or a combination of factors. Of course, those factors can result in interesting futures market investment strategies.

Booming bull markets dominated cotton futures in both 1973 and 1976, while bear markets were the case in the following years, 1974 and 1977. Price in cents per pound. (Chart by ContiCommodity Services Inc.)

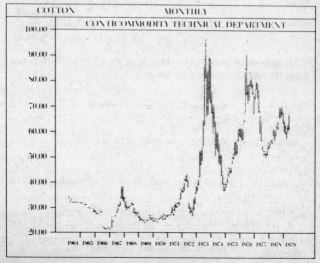

Planting of the crop generally begins in March and extends through May, and harvesting is done between August and December. To understand cotton investments fully, it is helpful to note what happens to the crop after it is harvested.

Harvested cotton is shipped to the gins, where it undergoes a cleaning procedure that strips away the fiber from the seed. In turn, the fiber, which is known as lint, then is pressed into the familiar bales of 500 pounds each. (The leftover cottonseed also is useful, and is processed into edible and industrial oil products.)

SOME OTHER FACTS ABOUT COTTON: China and Russia are the two biggest consumers of cotton. The United States ranks third. The cotton crop year runs from August 1 to July 31. The contract months for cotton futures are March, May, July, October, and December.

The Cotton Markets

Exchange	Size of Contract	Minimum Price Fluctuation	Daily Limit Price Fluctuations*
New York Cotton Exchange	50,000 pounds	1/100 cent per pound or $5 per contract	2 cents per pound ($1,000 per contract) compared with previous session's close

* If three or more contract months move the limit for three days in a row, the limit is raised to three cents.

PERIODIC REPORTS ON COTTON

U.S. Agricultural Marketing Service
   Cotton Price Statistics (monthly and annually)
U.S. Bureau of the Census
   Current Industrial Reports:
      Cotton Consumption and Stocks (monthly and annually)
U.S. Crop Reporting Board
   Crop Production (monthly and annually)
U.S. Economic Research Service
   Cotton and Wool Situation (five per year)

U.S. Foreign Agricultural Service
  Foreign Agriculture Circular, Cotton (irregular)

Foodstuffs

COFFEE

Any investor who has gone to the grocery store to buy
coffee in the past few years and seen the wide price swings
that have marked the product realizes how wild coffee
futures contracts have been over that period. From the
beginning of 1975 coffee futures prices on the New York
Coffee & Sugar Exchange climbed from about 60 cents per
pound to about $3.40 per pound by early 1977. From that
point, however, prices dropped back to near $1 a pound in
1978. That's a market in which fortunes can both be won
and lost quite easily.

*Coffee futures prices ended 1978 in a rather narrow trading range
before gaining some upward momentum in 1979. Price in cents
per pound. (Chart by Clayton Brokerage Co. of St. Louis)*

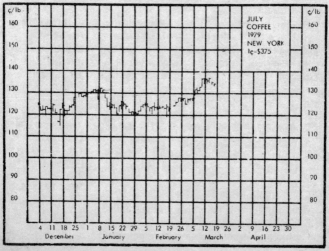

Coffee, unlike most futures market commodities, is somewhat more difficult to follow because nearly 80 percent of the world's coffee trees are located in Central and South America. And that makes the industry substantially more difficult to monitor than the U.S. orange industry, for instance. Moreover, the one-two punch of Brazil and Colombia together account for about 33 percent of the world's total coffee production. It's a situation similar to that surrounding the world's oil supply, where the countries making up the Organization of Petroleum Exporting Countries (OPEC) control so much of the world energy supplies. Thus, wild prices often are a distinguishing characteristic of the coffee market.

Interestingly, the United States is the world's largest consumer and importer of coffee. At the same time, the United States produces absolutely no coffee domestically.

SOME OTHER FACTS ABOUT COFFEE: The contract months for coffee futures are March, May, July, September, and December. Besides being used as a beverage and as a food flavoring, coffee and its derivative forms also are used in a variety of other products, such as soaps, paints, shoe polish, and medicine, all of which contain oil from the coffee bean.

The Coffee Markets

Exchange	Size of Contract	Minimum Price Fluctuation	Daily Limit Price Fluctuation
New York Coffee and Sugar Exchange (coffee "C")	37,500 pounds	1/100 cent per pound or $3.75 per contract	4 cents per pound ($1,500 per contract) compared with previous session's close
(coffee "B")	32,500 pounds	1/100 cent per pound or $3.25 per contract	4 cents per pound ($1,300 per contract) compared with previous session's close

COCOA

In many respects, cocoa futures may well be on the endangered-species list. Indeed, despite attempts by the New York Cocoa Exchange to make its product more attractive to investors, volume in cocoa contracts plunged sharply in recent years. In 1978, for example, activity on the exchange was down nearly 30 percent to 222,732 contracts from 307,681 a year before.

The decline in popularity is unfortunate for the crop, which until the past few years has enjoyed a long and rather distinguished history. Though native to Central and South America, cocoa was introduced into Europe as long ago as the 1400s. Today Africa also is a dominant force in the production of the beans. In fact, Africa currently ranks as the world's largest producer of the crop; the Chicago Board of Trade says the continent's production has ranged between 69 percent and 74 percent of total world output.

Among the African producers, about 33 percent of the crop comes from Ghana and some 20 percent from Nigeria. Other leading producers include Brazil, the Ivory Coast, Ecuador, the Dominican Republic, Venezuela, and Colombia. It's not difficult, therefore, to understand why statistics relating to the world's cocoa production are so difficult to come by and why the futures contracts on the crop have lost much of their investment appeal.

The situation in Ghana vividly illustrates this drawback. In that country, for example, the Ghana Cocoa Marketing Board, a government entity, makes the decision as to what percentage of the country's cocoa crop will be exported to other countries. Moreover, during the course of the year, that government body also distributes additional data such as crop estimates.

While raising of the cocoa tree primarily is centered in those countries noted above, the majority of the world's cocoa is consumed in Europe and the United States, with estimated shares of 60 percent and 20 percent, respectively. Some of the larger consumers include West Germany, the Netherlands, and the United Kingdom.

SOME OTHER FACTS ABOUT COCOA: Cocoa's crop year runs from October through September. During that year, however, two different crops are grown, the October–March main crop, which comprises about 80 percent of

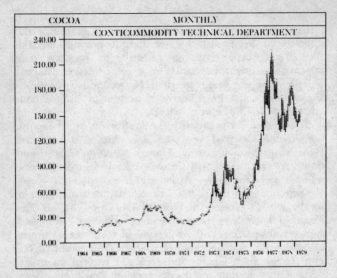

The period from 1973 to 1977 was especially good for cocoa futures prices, but it has been mostly downhill since. Price in cents per pound. (Chart by ContiCommodity Services Inc.)

production, and the May–June mid-crop, which makes up the remainder. Cocoa futures also are traded on the London Cocoa Terminal Market. On the New York Cocoa Exchange, the delivery months are December, March, May, July, and September.

The Cocoa Markets

Exchange	Size of Contract	Minimum Price Fluctuation	Daily Limit Price Fluctuations
New York Cocoa Exchange	30,000 pounds	1/100 cent per pound or $3 per contract	Six cents per pound ($1,800 per contract) compared with previous session's close

FROZEN CONCENTRATED ORANGE JUICE

Despite orange juice's appearance, the market for futures traded on the frozen concentrate nevertheless has a history of being rather thin. Therefore, orange-juice futures are not a suitable investment for all. Many commodity professionals tell story after story about how the orange-juice market has reacted in the past to a piece of news and run in price in one direction for day after day, not enabling investors to liquidate their positions. The fact that most of the oranges are grown in Florida makes trading in these futures even more hazardous. That is because damage to the Florida crop, or inclement weather conditions in that state, often cannot be offset by differing supply-and-demand considerations elsewhere in the country.

Yet, despite these caveats, the orange-juice market has provided a great deal of opportunity for profit in the past few years. Indeed, from 1975 to autumn of 1977, prices rose on the New York Cotton Exchange to more than $1.30 a pound from about 50 cents a pound. In 1978, however, prices were hit hard by a January freeze in Florida which sharply curtailed crop expectations.

The market for futures on frozen concentrated orange juice is relatively young, having been introduced by the New York Cotton Exchange only in 1966 although the actual concept of frozen concentrated orange juice came into prominence in this country during the late 1940s when electric freezers replaced those familiar old ice boxes.

Moreover, frozen concentrated orange juice is very much an American product, with the United States producing about 33 percent of the world's total supply, and consuming nearly all of its own production. Of the U.S. output, Florida supplies about three-fourths and California about one-fifth, with Arizona and Texas making up the rest. (Florida also supplies about 25 percent of the world's oranges.) About 72 percent of Florida's annual orange crop is processed into the frozen concentrate.

SOME OTHER FACTS ABOUT ORANGE JUICE: The contract months for frozen concentrated orange-juice futures are January, March, April, May, and November. The crop year runs from December through November. In Florida, the harvest begins in December and usually is finished sometime in June. Orange trees must grow for at least four years before they begin to produce fruit. A five-year-old tree will yield just one box of oranges a year, while trees that are between twenty and forty-five years old generally yield about six times as much.

The Orange Juice Markets

Exchange	Size of Contract	Minimum Price Fluctuation	Daily Limit Price Fluctuations*
New York Cotton Exchange	15,000 pounds of orange solids	5/100 cent per pound or $7.50 per contract	Three cents a pound ($450 per contract) compared with the previous session's close

* The limit is raised to five cents a pound when three or more contract months close at the limit in the same direction for five days in a row.

SUGAR

When it comes to boasting of colorful histories, most other commodities on which futures contracts are traded can't compare with sugar. The rise to power of Fidel Castro in Cuba during the late 1950s–early 1960s sent sugar prices on a roller-coaster ride that made sugar futures one of the most spectacular speculative plays around.

Yet that roller-coaster ride has evened off somewhat in the past three years. Between 1976 and 1978, sugar prices moved in a rather narrow range of less than 10 cents a pound. That differed sharply from late 1974 to early 1975, when futures quotes surged more than 50 cents a pound on the New York Coffee & Sugar Exchange.

Though sugar actually is derived both from beet sugar and cane sugar, more than half the world's output comes from the bamboolike sugar-cane plant. Harvested usually in late winter and spring, U.S. sugar production is con-

The late 1974–early 1975 period clearly stands out as the most exciting era for that contract in the past fifteen years. Prices in cents per pound. (Chart by ContiCommodity Services Inc.)

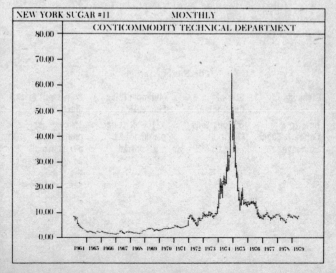

fined for the most part to the semitropical-weather states of Florida, Hawaii, and Louisiana. The top beet-sugar states, meanwhile, are Idaho and Colorado. Sugar beets are planted in the spring and harvest occurs by late fall or early winter.

Internationally, the United States ranks third behind the Soviet Union and Cuba in terms of sugar produced annually. This country is one of the few countries which produces sugar from both types of plants. The other leading sugar-producing nations include Brazil, India, Mexico, France, the Philippines, Poland, and Australia. Though about 70 percent of all sugar produced is consumed in the country where it is grown, the rising demand for sugar has resulted in large imports of the product by many countries in recent years. The United States, for example, is one of the world's largest importers of sugar, its annual per-capita consumption of 100 pounds creating an enormous sweet tooth that needs to be nurtured. As would be expected, the United States, therefore, exports very little raw sugar.

SOME OTHER FACTS ABOUT SUGAR: A sugar-cane plant can be harvested eighteen months after planting, and then continues to produce for several years. The trading months for sugar futures in the United States are January, March, May, July, September, and October. In addition to the New York market, sugar futures also are traded in London and Paris.

The Sugar Markets

Exchange	Size of Contract	Minimum Price Fluctuation	Daily Limit Price Fluctuations
New York Coffee & Sugar Exchange	50 long tons (112,000 pounds)	1/100 cent per pound or $11.20 per contract	½ cent per pound ($560 per contract) compared with the previous session's close

POTATOES

At one time, potato futures were among the most popular of all contracts making up this nation's futures markets. However, in the past few years the potato sector of the market has been struck with several near-disasters which have driven many investors away from the potato contract and have heaped financial woes on the country's major potato futures market, the New York Mercantile Exchange.

During 1979 the potato futures market was dealt a stunning blow when several truckloads of Maine potatoes failed federal inspection in New York City, causing the New York Merc to halt trading in a number of contracts. Unfortunately for the Merc, the occurrence reminded many people of the infamous potato debacle of several years earlier which was precipitated by two large Western potato producers defaulting on a huge commitment of potatoes. So, while the circumstances were different in the second case, the uproar that followed nevertheless caused many traders to back away from the potato markets and renewed the call by many market critics that futures contracts on potatoes be outlawed.

To rectify the situation somewhat, the New York Mercantile, as of this writing, was working hard to amend its potato contract so that it would not be based solely on the type of potato grown in Maine. Instead, it was rewriting its contract specifications so that all fall-harvested round white potatoes would qualify as deliverable against the contracts traded on its floor.

The Chicago Mercantile Exchange, meanwhile, which trades contracts on the less-popular Russet Burbank type of potato grown mostly in Idaho, also was taking steps to spur renewed interest in potato futures. Yet the CME's needs are far less than the New York Merc, whose entire existence is threatened by the fall-off in trading that has resulted from the potato scandals.

SOME OTHER FACTS ABOUT POTATOES: In the United States, the greatest demand for potatoes is for potato chips, shoestring potatoes, and frozen and dehydrated products. Over the past ten years, there has been a significant decline in the amount of potatoes consumed as a fresh vegetable as the various other forms grew in popularity. The contract months for potatoes on both exchanges are January, March, April, May, and November.

The Potato Markets*

Exchange	Size of Contract	Minimum Price Fluctuation	Daily Limit Price Fluctuation
New York Mercantile Exchange	50,000 pounds	1 cent per 100 pounds or $5 per contract	50 cents per 100 pounds ($250 per contract) compared with the previous session's close
Chicago Mercantile Exchange	80,000 pounds	1 cent per 100 pounds or $8 per contract	50 cents per 100 pounds ($400 per contract) compared with the previous session's close

* At the time of this writing, the exchanges were altering the specifications for their contracts. To keep abreast of the changes, consult the exchanges or your broker.

PERIODIC REPORTS ON FOODSTUFFS

U.S. Agricultural Marketing Service
   Sugar and Sweetener Report (monthly)
U.S. Crop Reporting Board
   Citrus Fruits (annually)
   Cold Storage (monthly and annually)
   Crop Production (monthly and annually)
   Potato Stocks (four per year)
   Potatoes and Sweet potatoes (annually)
U.S. Economic Research Service
   Fruit Situation (quarterly)
U.S. Foreign Agricultural Service
   Foreign Agriculture Circulars:
      Cocoa (irregularly)
      Coffee (irregularly)
      Fresh and Processed Citrus Fruits (irregularly)
      Sugar (irregularly)
Gill and Duffus, New York, N.Y.
   Cocoa Statistics (annually)

Poultry Commodities

FRESH EGGS

An agricultural product with a long history, fresh eggs, along with their counterpart in the futures market's poultry sector, iced broilers, have captured the imagination of many investors, both for their dynamic price movements as well as their cyclical tendencies.

The movement of egg prices over the past three years illustrates this vividly. In January 1976 the average wholesale price of large white eggs was 70 cents a dozen, according to the Agriculture Marketing Service of the United States Agriculture Department. By April, however, the price had fallen to less than 59 cents a dozen. But prices subsequently turned around sharply and by year-end stood at more than 82 cents a dozen. The same was true in 1977, when prices roamed within a range of 53 cents a dozen and 79 cents a dozen, and in 1978, when the span was 49 cents a dozen to 73 cents a dozen. Such volatility makes the fresh-egg market especially attractive to futures market speculators.

Yet that degree of volatility requires that traders be especially keen to market changes and to the degree of exposure inherent in their market positions. That is because once prices in the egg market break, and begin to head downward, the rule of thumb always has been that an extended decline is in the making. A warning: The conventional wisdom for some investments, especially stocks, allows that one should "hold on during a decline because the market will turn around and come back." That adage is not applicable in the fresh-egg market.

The egg-production industry is a business with wide appeal throughout the United States. According to the Chicago Board of Trade, the South Atlantic states account for the largest chunk, with 26 percent of the total market. Yet California is the largest single producer, with a market share of about 14 percent.

The egg-production business is not as simple as most novices seem to believe. For example, chickens that are bred especially to produce eggs will begin to lay at about twenty weeks of age. Within a year or so they usually will reach their top production efficiency, which may be as high as 350 eggs a year. However, at that point problems usually develop, and the farmer has to make a decision. After that first year, the chicken's egg production declines sharply, and the farmer must decide whether to sell the chicken for slaughter, as its feed costs no longer are justified economically, or whether he should put it into forced molting.

In forced molting, the farmer stops feeding the hen, which then goes into a state of shock accompanied by a loss of feathers. As soon as that happens, heavy feeding is reinstituted, and the hen soon regains much of its laying capability, as much as 95 percent in some cases. By using such methods, therefore, the productive life of most hens can be extended to about three years.

SOME OTHER FACTS ABOUT FRESH EGGS: Traditionally, the egg market has been a very seasonal business, with the hot summer months usually resulting in hens laying fewer eggs, both because of the heat and because of their reduced appetites. But that has changed radically in recent times due to better diets as well as newer climate-controlled laying houses. All months qualify as contract months for fresh eggs.

The Egg Markets

Exchange	Size of Contract	Minimum Price Fluctuation	Daily Limit Price Fluctuations
Chicago Mercantile Exchange	750 cases of 30 dozen eggs each	$.0005 per dozen or $11.25 per contract	Two cents per dozen ($450 per contract) compared with previous session's close

ICED BROILERS

The other half of the poultry daily double, iced broilers, the small two-to-four-pound chickens sold in supermarkets, have achieved phenomenal growth in consumption over recent years, thanks in large part to such luminaries as Colonel Sanders and Frank Purdue. In 1940, total United States production of broiler chickens aggregated just 413 million pounds for the year; in 1978, meanwhile, output had skyrocketed all the way up to about 14 billion pounds. The business is no longer the Mom-and-Pop operation it once was.

And that growing popularity of the product, as well as its ever-increasing production numbers, has resulted in futures contracts on iced broilers becoming a very attractive investment medium for many futures market speculators. In 1976, for example, wholesale chicken prices vacillated between about 35 cents a pound and 44 cents a pound; in 1977 between 36 cents a pound and 44 cents a pound; and in 1978 between 40 cents a pound and 50 cents a pound.

Basically, the broiler-chicken industry is limited to the Southeastern and Middle Atlantic sections of the United States. Included among the top-producing states are Alabama, Arkansas, Delaware, Georgia, Maine, Maryland, Mississippi, North Carolina, and Virginia.

Those chicks which are earmarked to be broilers generally mature to their desired weight in just about nine weeks. At that point they are shipped to processing plants for slaughter, and within a few days after slaughter are found on the shelf in the supermarket.

One of the major considerations that investors should consider when mulling investments in this area is the general health of the country's economy, or more specifically, the impact inflation may be having on household budgets. When meat prices rise, for example, the odds are good that more and more shoppers at the supermarket will opt for an extra chicken meal that week to counteract the high price of beef. Such supply-and-demand considerations cannot always be detected from the production data supplied regularly in the futures market, but nevertheless play a huge role in determining the attractiveness of an investment.

SOME OTHER FACTS ABOUT ICED BROILERS: Demand for iced broilers is highly seasonal, with peaks in the summertime (barbecuing) and regular occurrences at holidays. There are two exceptions, however: Thanksgiving and Christmas, when turkeys are preferred. The contract months for iced broilers are January, April, May, June, July, August, September, October, November, and December.

The Iced-Broiler Markets

Exchange	Size of Contract	Minimum Price Fluctuation	Daily Limit Price Fluctuations
Chicago Board of Trade	30,000 pounds	2.5 cents per 100 pounds or $7.50 per contract	$2 per 100 pounds ($600 per contract) compared with the previous session's close

PERIODIC REPORTS ON POULTRY

U.S. Crop Reporting Board
    Cold Storage (monthly and annually)
    Eggs, Chickens and Turkeys (monthly)
    Poultry Slaughter (monthly and annually)
U.S. Economic Research Service
    Poultry and Egg Situation (five per year)
    Poultry Market Statistics (annually)
U.S. Foreign Agricultural Service
    Foreign Agriculture Circular, Poultry and Eggs (irregularly)
National Broiler Council, Washington, D.C.
    Washington Report (biweekly)
Poultry and Egg Institute of America, Kansas City, Mo.
    Hot Line (weekly)

Livestock Commodities

BEEF

Perhaps nothing is more natural than trading futures on a commodity such as beef, which is extremely familiar to all Americans and which historically has undergone many very interesting and volatile price swings. On a per-capita basis, America ranks right near the top of the list when it comes to demand for red meat.

In fact, 1978 was a perfect example of the surging interest that is being exhibited in the cattle market. According to the Economic Research Service of the United States Department of Agriculture, average retail beef prices, comprising all major cuts, climbed sharply during the year. In January, for instance, prices stood at about $1.59 a pound, and then rose steadily until June, when they reached almost to the $2-a-pound level. And though they dropped back somewhat from that level over the re-

Live cattle futures prices were in a prolonged bull market from late 1977 into mid-1979. Price in cents per pound. (Chart by ContiCommodity Services Inc.)

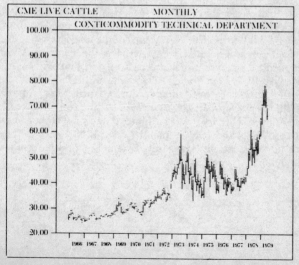

mainder of the year, the price performance nevertheless resulted in a boom year in cattle futures trading.

Because of the wide-ranging demand for beef in this country, the business is an extremely important one in those states that account for the majority of the country's beef production. They include Texas, Iowa, Nebraska, Kansas, Oklahoma, South Dakota, California, Missouri, Illinois, and Montana.

In evaluating beef futures investments, it is extremely important that the prospective investor understand all the components involved in bringing cattle to market. Obviously, production is affected by a number of factors, but one of the most important is the feeding costs required to raise calves. Because corn is the major feed for cattle, both corn production and corn prices must be analyzed in depth to correctly evaluate the cattle-market situation.

Moreover, the federal government plays a very large role in the cattle business, and not just in the most obvious inspecting and grading duties. For example, the government has a hand in acreage controls each year—which can affect the corn-feed atmosphere—as well as having overseeing duties in relation to export quotas for beef to be shipped overseas.

SOME OTHER FACTS ABOUT BEEF: The Chicago Mercantile Exchange, the nation's second-largest futures mart, trades three beef contracts: live beef cattle, boneless beef, and feeder cattle. The New York Mercantile Exchange has a contract in imported lean beef. On the Chicago Merc, the contract months for boneless beef are January, February, April, June, August, October, and December; for feeder cattle they are January, March, April, May, August, September, October, and November; and for live cattle they are February, April, June, August, October, and December. The contract months on the New York Merc are January, March, May, July, September, and November.

The Beef Markets

Exchange	Size of Contract	Minimum Price Fluctuation	Daily Limit Price Fluctuations
Chicago Mercantile Exchange (live beef cattle)	40,000 pounds	$.025 per pound or $10 per contract	1½ cents per pound ($600 per contract) compared with previous session's close
Chicago Mercantile Exchange (live feeder cattle)	42,000 pounds	$.025 per pound or $10.50 per contract	1½ cents per pound ($630 per contract) compared with previous session's close
Chicago Mercantile Exchange (boneless beef)	38,000 pounds	$.025 per pound or $9.50 per contract	1½ cents per pound ($570 per contract) compared with previous session's close
New York Mercantile Exchange (imported lean beef)	36,000 pounds	$.02 per 100 pounds or $7.20 per contract	1½ cents per pound ($540 per contract) compared with previous session's close

PORK

Though commodities comprising the pork sector of the futures market are some of the most popular and rewarding investment vehicles in all of the markets, they nevertheless also are some of the most misunderstood. Jokes about pork-belly futures have become almost commonplace in American culture. Even a fairly successful movie of a few years back, "For Pete's Sake," starring Barbra Streisand, used investing in pork-belly futures as one of the comedic points of the story.

For the record, pork bellies are that section of the underside of a hog which ultimately becomes cured sliced bacon. As such, they account for some 15 percent of the total weight of a hog. But by no means is the pork belly the only important part of a hog. Other cuts such as chops, loins, hams, and butts also account for major pork products and are in great demand by the public. As a result, hogs are represented in the futures markets not only by pork-belly contracts but also by contracts on live hogs.

As with beef cattle, the cost of feeding hogs constitutes a very important variable to consider in raising hogs for the marketplace. Therefore, the majority of hog production in this country is centered in the Corn Belt. In fact, more than half of the United States' production comes from four states: Iowa, Illinois, Indiana, and Missouri. But a significant number of hogs also are raised elsewhere, including Minnesota, Nebraska, Ohio, Wisconsin, South Dakota, Georgia, Kansas, and North Carolina.

Because demand for pork products has risen sharply over the years in response to a growing acceptance of the meat by a wider audience of consumers plus the impact inflation has had on the prices of other meats, pork has been a very interesting futures market play. In 1976, for example, the average retail price of pork ranged between $1.17 a pound and $1.44 a pound; in 1977 between $1.19 a pound and $1.30 a pound; and in 1978 between $1.33 a pound and $1.50 a pound. Such movements provide ample investment opportunities.

With pork, both demand and supply considerations follow highly seasonal patterns. On the supply side, the majority of farrowings, or pig births, occur during March, April, and May. Those animals, termed spring pigs, would

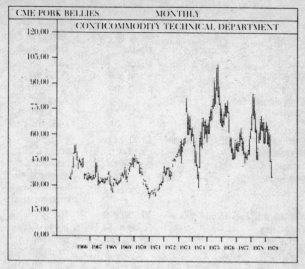

The highly volatile market for pork-belly futures was especially evident in the 1970s, when surging inflation significantly affected food prices. Price in cents per pound. (Chart by ContiCommodity Services Inc.)

come to market during the August-through-December period. Accordingly, prices tend to be lower during that period, which in large part accounts for the greater demand consumers exhibit for pork products during those months.

SOME OTHER FACTS ABOUT PORK: Pork bellies continue to be one of the most exciting products in the commodities market because of the relative strength of the end product, bacon. Historically, despite major price increases, the public's appetite for bacon never ebbs. In large part, that is because there is no substitute product for bacon on the breakfast tables of many Americans. The contract months for live hogs are February, April, June, July, August, October, and December. For frozen pork bellies they are February, March, May, July, and August.

The Pork Markets

Exchange	Size of Contract	Minimum Price Fluctuation	Daily Limit Price Fluctuations
Chicago Mercantile Exchange (frozen pork bellies)	38,000 pounds	$0.00025 per pound or $9.50 per contract	$0.02 per pound ($760 per contract) compared with the previous session's close
Chicago Mercantile Exchange (live hogs)	30,000 pounds	$0.00025 per pound or $7.50 per contract	$0.015 per pound ($450 per contract) compared with the previous session's close
MidAmerica Commodity Exchange (live hogs)	15,000 pounds	$0.00025 per pound or $3.75 per contract	$0.015 per pound ($225 per contract) compared with the previous session's close

PERIODIC REPORTS ON LIVESTOCK

U.S. Agricultural Marketing Service
   Livestock, Meat, Wool Market News (weekly)
U.S. Crop Reporting Board
   Cattle on Feed (monthly and annually)
   Cold Storage (monthly and annually)
   Hogs and Pigs (quarterly)
   Livestock Slaughter (monthly and annually)
   Meat Animals (annually)
U.S. Economic Service
   Dairy Situation (five per year)
   Livestock and Meat Situation (bimonthly)
   Livestock and Meat Statistics (annually)
U.S. Foreign Agricultural Service
   Foreign Agriculture Circular, Livestock and Meat (irregularly)

Metal Commodities

GOLD

The most visible and closely watched commodity on which futures contracts are based, gold also is one of the least-difficult commodities around on which to predict future prices trends. At least that has been the case during the decade of the 1970s, when economic upheaval throughout the world, runaway inflation, and a sharply sagging United States dollar threw the world's economic order into chaos. For when it comes to gold, one thing is certain: the metal is the obverse of the United States' monetary and economic health. When the country's economic woes translate into a declining U.S. currency, as has been the case for much of recent history, gold is always the beneficiary.

That certainly has been evident in the performance of gold in the period from 1976 to 1979. Between the summer of 1976 and the summer of 1979, for example, gold skyrocketed in price from less than $110 an ounce to more than $310 an ounce as the United States was ravaged by event after event, such as two gasoline shortages, the expectation of recession in late 1979–early 1980, and double-digit inflation.

Thus, as the saying goes, "In times of troubles investors flock to gold." And they have. In large numbers. And many of them are earning huge profits in the process.

Gold's price is "fixed" twice each day in London, where members of the gold market meet to set a price that satisfies both buyers and sellers. While actual gold transactions often are priced outside these fixings, actions of this London price-fixing group effectively set a "benchmark" standard from which foreign-exchange traders, futures traders, and all other types of investors, speculators, and financial institutions can make their investment decisions.

Nearly 70 percent of all the new gold produced worldwide annually comes from the gold-bearing reefs off the coast of South Africa. While there are several other countries that contribute to the annual output, such as the Soviet Union, Canada, the United States, Ghana, Australia, Rhodesia, and the Philippines, their paltry production numbers pale in contrast to the massive output of South Africa.

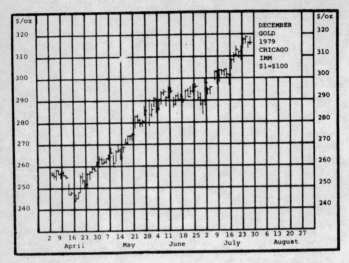

The steep inflation, and prospects for a recession, drove gold's price up sharply during the middle months of 1979. Price in dollars per ounce. (Chart by Clayton Brokerage Co. of St. Louis)

SOME OTHER FACTS ABOUT GOLD: The United States holds a larger reserve of gold within its borders than any other country, with its vaults at Fort Knox, Kentucky, and the Federal Reserve Bank in New York filled to capacity. On the MidAmerica and New York Mercantile exchanges the contract months for gold are March, June, September, and December. On the Commodity Exchange Inc. they are February, April, June, August, October, and December. On the Chicago Board of Trade they are January, March, May, June, July, September, and November. And on the Chicago Mercantile Exchange they are March, June, September, and December.

The Gold Markets

Exchange	Size of Contract	Minimum Price Fluctuation	Daily Limit Price Fluctuations
Commodity Exchange Inc.	100 troy ounces	10 cents per troy ounce or $10 per contract	$10 per troy ounce ($1,000 a contract) compared with the previous session's close
Chicago Mercantile Exchange	100 troy ounces	10 cents per troy ounce or $10 per contract	$10 per troy ounce ($1,000 a contract) compared with the previous session's close
MidAmerica Commodity Exchange	33.2 troy ounces	2½ cents per troy ounce or 83 cents per contract	$10 per troy ounce ($321.50 per contract) compared with the previous session's close
Chicago Board of Trade	3 kilograms	10 cents an ounce or $9.60 per contract	$10 an ounce ($960 per contract) compared with the previous session's close
New York Mercantile Exchange	32.15 troy ounces	10 cents per troy ounce or $3.21 per contract	$10 per troy ounce ($321.50 per contract) compared with the previous session's close

PLATINUM AND PALLADIUM

Platinum and what? That's the question you may ask when reading the heading on this next group of commodities. The word is palladium, one of the six metals that comprise the "platinum" group of metals. It's also one which because of its similar properties of electrical conductivity often is used in conjunction or interchangeably with the more popularly known platinum.

But just because most people do not know what palladium is does not mean that the futures contracts on that metal have not proven to be highly attractive speculative vehicles over the years. Indeed, while precious metals such as gold, silver, and platinum generally respond to economic events in approximately the same fashion and to similar degrees, palladium has shown repeatedly that its price movements often are more extreme and the time

The past two years have seen platinum prices rise sharply to a point where they are about four times what they were seven years before. Price in dollars per ounce. (Chart by ContiCommodity Services Inc.)

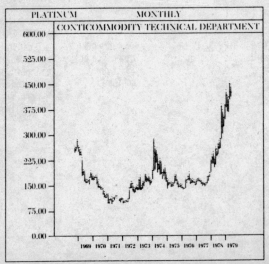

periods in which its quotes tend higher or lower also generally do not follow the pattern of the other metals.

Because of the excellent conductivity of the two metals, both platinum and palladium have wide usage in the manufacture of telephone and other communication equipment and industrial controls. Yet their largest use probably is in the industrial chemical industries, where the metals are employed as catalysts in producing nitric acid, which is a very important component of both fertilizer and explosives.

Both also are used widely in producing gasoline and other propane products. Moreover, they have become even more important in recent years because of the growing ecological concern over automobile emissions. Platinum and palladium have enjoyed increased demand because they are used in the catalytic converters that the federal government has mandated must be on this nation's cars to protect against excessive emissions of carbon monoxide and hydrocarbons.

SOME OTHER FACTS ABOUT PLATINUM AND PALLADIUM: South Africa, Canada, the Soviet Union, and Colombia are the world's largest producers of the "platinum group" of metals. Because the United States' domestic production is extremely small, this country historically has been a net importer of the metals. The contract months for platinum are January, April, July, and October plus three current months. For palladium they are March, June, September, and December, plus three current months.

The Platinum and Palladium Markets

Exchange	Size of Contract	Minimum Price Fluctuation	Daily Limit Price Fluctuations
New York Mercantile Exchange (platinum)	50 troy ounces	10 cents per troy ounce or $5 per contract	$10 per troy ounce ($500 a contract) compared with the previous session's close
New York Mercantile Exchange (palladium)	100 troy ounces	5 cents per troy ounce or $5 per contract	$10 per troy ounce ($1,000 per contract) compared with the previous session's close

SILVER AND SILVER COINS

As rampant inflation has eaten away at both the savings and earnings of many Americans over the decade of the 1970s, a great number of investors have turned away from "traditional" investment strategies for the speculative plays of precious metals. While actual ownership of silver is one way to accomplish this end, playing futures contracts in metals such as silver and silver coins is another. And for those investors who have opted for silver futures, there has been sufficient opportunity for reward. On the New York Commodity Exchange Inc., for example, silver futures prices rose from about the $4.20-an-ounce level in mid-1976 to more than $11.00 an ounce in mid-1979.

While the word silver immediately sparks thoughts of jewelry and ornaments, less than 10 percent of the world's silver output is used for such applications. Instead, the

Silver futures prices approached the $10-an-ounce level midway through 1979, in large part because of investors' disenchantment with traditional investment vehicles. Price in cents per ounce. (Chart by Clayton Brokerage Co. of St. Louis)

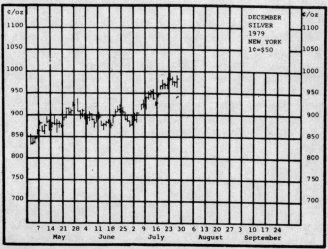

vast majority of the world's silver production is used industrially, as in photographic film, plates, sensitized papers, and photocopying machines. In addition, the metal has wide acceptance in the electrical and electronic industries because of its heat-and-rust-resistant properties.

Of total world production, nearly three-fourths of all silver is produced in the Western Hemisphere, with Canada, Peru, Mexico, and the United States the leading producers. In the United States, for example, about 99 percent of domestic silver production is utilized for industrial uses.

Interestingly, the largest source of silver is not the silver-mining. Instead, the largest providers of the world's silver are the base-metal ores copper, lead, and zinc. Because silver can be produced as a byproduct in the refining of these metals, supply-and-demand considerations in those markets also play a very important role in judging prospective silver investments. Arizona, Montana, Utah, and Colorado are among the leading states producing silver.

SOME OTHER FACTS ABOUT SILVER: The growing popularity in recent years of commemorative coin sets and plates sets has increased the demand equation for silver in this country. While that market still is relatively small in relation to the overall demand picture, it nevertheless raises interesting possibilities about the silver market for the future. The contract months for silver coins on the New York Merc are January, April, July, and October plus three current months, and on the Chicago Merc are March, June, September, and December. For silver futures on the Comex they are January, March, May, July, September, and December; on the Chicago Board of Trade they are February, April, May, June, August, September, and December; and on the MidAmerica they are February, April, June, August, October, and December.

The Silver Markets

Exchange	Size of Contract	Minimum Price Fluctuation	Daily Limit Price Fluctuations
New York Mercantile Exchange (silver coins)	10 bags of $1,000 face value each	$1 per bag or $10 a contract	$150 per bag ($1,500 per contract) compared with the previous session's close
Chicago Mercantile Exchange (silver coins)	5 bags of $1,000 face value each	$1 per bag or $5 a contract	$150 per bag ($750 per contract) compared with the previous session's close
MidAmerica Commodity Exchange (silver coins)	5 bags of $1,000 face value each	$1 per bag or $5 a contract	$150 per bag ($750 per contract) compared with the previous session's close
Commodity Exchange Inc. (silver)	5,000 troy ounces	1/10 cent per troy ounce or $5 per contract	20 cents per ounce ($1,000 per contract) compared with the previous session's close
Chicago Board of Trade (silver)	5,000 troy ounces	1/10 cent per troy ounce or $5 per contract	20 cents per ounce ($1,000 per contract) compared with the previous session's close
MidAmerica Commodity Exchange (silver)	1,000 troy ounces	$0.05 per troy ounce or $5 per contract	20 cents per ounce ($200 per contract) compared with the previous session's close

COPPER

The copper industry is one of the most important businesses in this country. It is also one in which the federal government plays a very large assistance role. It does so by promoting increased production of this valuable metal through a variety of ways, including production-expansion assistance loans, accelerated rates for amortization of capital investments, and controls on imports and exports.

With so much input into this market, therefore, copper futures have become an extremely popular investment vehicle because of the wide price swings that have resulted from such outside influences. In early 1975, for example, copper futures prices on the New York Commodity Exchange stood at about 52 cents a pound. A few months later they were up near 60 cents a pound and then fell back down to 52 cents a pound just a few months after that. By mid-1976 prices were approaching 78 cents a pound, yet three months later they were back down in the low 50-cent area. And that pattern has continued ever since.

Copper is extremely important to this country because of its wide variety of uses. More than half of all copper demand, for example, comes from the electrical and electronic industries, which need copper for products such as motors, generators, fans, and industrial controls. Copper also is found widely in communications equipment such as telephones and communications satellites as well as in almost every home appliance. The United States is the world's largest producer of copper, accounting for nearly one-fourth of the world's output. Other large producers include the Soviet Union, Canada, Chile, Zambia, and Zaire.

Within the United States, the mining industry offers an intriguing display of market concentration as more than 90 percent of the country's copper-mine production comes out of just five Western states: Arizona, Utah, New Mexico, Montana, and Nevada. The copper-smelting industry, however, is largely based on the East Coast, with most of the smelting taking place in New York, New Jersey, and Maryland.

SOME OTHER FACTS ABOUT COPPER: Because copper is a base-metal ore and contains certain quantities of other valuable minerals such as gold, silver, nickel, iron, lead,

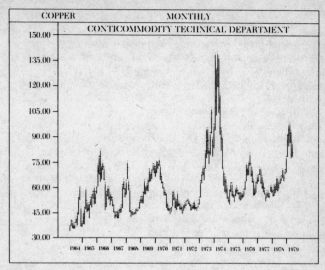

Copper futures prices have been extremely volatile over the past fifteen years, making the contract especially attractive to speculators. Price in cents per pound. (Chart by ContiCommodity Services Inc.)

zinc, platinum, and palladium the supply-and-demand considerations of those products must also be considered in evaluating copper investments. The contract months for copper futures on the Comex are January, March, May, July, September, and December.

The Copper Markets

Exchange	Size of Contract	Minimum Price Fluctuation	Daily Limit Price Fluctuations
Commodity Exchange Inc.	25,000 pounds	5/100 cents per pound or $12.50 per contract	Three cents a pound ($750 per contract) compared with the previous session's close

PERIODIC REPORTS ON METALS

U.S. Bureau of Mines
  Mineral Industry Surveys, Copper (monthly)
  Mineral Industry Surveys, Gold and Silver Monthly
    (monthly)
  Mineral Industry Surveys, Platinum Group Metals (quar-
    terly)
  Minerals Yearbook (annually)
U.S. Bureau of the Mint
  Annual Report of the Director (annually)
American Metal Market, New York, N.Y. (daily)
J. Aron & Co., New York, N.Y.
  Annual Review and Outlook, Metal Markets (annually)
  Gold Statistics and Analysis (annually)
  Monthly Review (monthly)
  Silver Statistics and Analysis (annually)
Handy and Harman, New York, N.Y.
  The Silver Market (annually)

Financial Instruments

FOREIGN CURRENCIES

It makes a lot of sense. The inflation that has marked the decade of the 1970s and which has wreaked economic havoc on nations across the world has made the market for foreign-currency futures an exciting and dynamic arena both for speculation and hedging.

Any American who has sat in front of his television set to hear Walter Cronkite report on the continuing deterioration of the United States dollar, or who has read about the great concern that decline is causing in Washington, realizes that the futures markets for foreign currencies offer unique opportunities.

In starting up trading in foreign currencies in 1972, the Chicago Mercantile Exchange surely realized what vibrant and popular investment vehicles these contracts could be. But exchange officials probably had no idea just how popular they would become. Indeed, the growth of currency futures volume is one of the reasons why financial-instrument futures in general have been growing at a much more rapid pace than agricommodity futures in the past few years.

To understand the profit possibilities in currency futures, simply take a look at the table, "Exchange Rate Versus the U.S. Dollar," which documents the changes the United States dollar underwent in 1978.

Exchange Rate Versus the U.S. Dollar

Currency	January	June	December
Japanese Yen	240.974	214.303	196.105
West German Mark	2.1186	2.0845	1.8795
Swiss Franc	1.9913	1.8853	1.6740
Canadian Dollar	1.1008	1.1216	1.1797
British Pound	1.9321	1.8363	1.9844
Mexican Peso	22.7450	22.7948	22.7557

It's obvious that the opportunities are there for the investor who can correctly forecast the direction of exchange rates. Yet, a word of caution before you set out to get rich by predicting in which direction the dollar is headed. A number of varying factors account for the

movement of currencies relative to other currencies. A
great deal of research should be undertaken, and a sound
conclusion reached, before setting out on this course.

SOME OTHER FACTS ABOUT CURRENCY FUTURES: The
Chicago Mercantile Exchange has contracts in eight foreign
currencies: British pounds, Canadian dollars, Dutch guilders, West German marks, French francs, Japanese yen,
Mexican pesos, and Swiss francs. The New York Mercantile
Exchange lists contracts in West German marks, Canadian
dollars, Swiss francs, British pounds, and Japanese yen.
(Currently neither the Dutch guilder nor the French franc
are traded often enough to provide any concrete information.)

The Foreign Currency Markets

Exchange	Size of Contract	Minimum Price Fluctuation	Daily Limit Price Fluctuation
Chicago Mercantile Exchange (British pound)	25,000 BP	$.005 per pound or $12.50 per contract	$.0500 per pound ($1,250 per contract) compared with the previous session's close
(Canadian dollar)	100,000 CD	$.0001 per Canadian dollar or $10 per contract	$.0075 per Canadian dollar ($750 per contract) compared with the previous session's close
(West German mark)	125,000 DM	$.0001 per mark or $12.50 per contract	$.01 per mark ($1,250 per contract) compared with the previous session's close
(Japanese yen)	12,500,000 Y	$.000001 per yen or $12.50 per contract	$.015 per yen ($1,500 per contract) compared with the previous session's close

Exchange	Size of Contract	Minimum Price Fluctuation	Daily Limit Price Fluctuation
(Mexican peso)	1,000,000 P	$.00001 per peso or $10 per contract	$.00150 per peso ($1,500 per contract) compared with the previous session's close
(Swiss franc)	125,000 SF	$.0001 per franc or $12.50 per contract	$.0150 per franc ($1,875 per contract) compared with the previous session's close
New York Mercantile Exchange (West German mark)	125,000 DM	$.0001 per mark or $12.50 per contract	$.01 per mark ($1,250 per contract) compared with the previous session's close
(Canadian dollar)	100,000 CD	$.0001 per Canadian dollar or $10 per contract	$.0075 per Canadian dollar ($750 per contract) compared with the previous session's close
(Swiss franc)	125,000 SF	$.0001 per franc or $12.50 per contract	$.01 per franc ($1,250 per contract) compared with the previous session's close
(British pound)	25,000 BP	$.0005 per pound or $12.50 per contract	$.0500 per pound ($1,250 per contract) compared with the previous session's close
(Japanese yen)	12,500,000 Y	$.000001 per yen or $12.50 per contract	$.0100 per yen ($1,250 per contract) compared with the previous session's close

INTEREST RATES

Like foreign currencies, the market for futures contracts on interest rates definitely is a market for the 1980s because of the sharply changing economies of the world. As a result, more and more new contracts tied to interest-rate movements are being developed on a regular basis by the nation's futures exchanges. In addition, new exchanges such as the Amex Commodities Exchange and the New York Futures Exchange are being created just to satisfy a part of the ever-growing appetite for interest-rate futures.

Various types of securities make up the interest-rate sector of the futures market. The most widely recognized ones, probably, are the three types of debt obligation issued by the United States Treasury Department. They are Treasury bills, which are short-term (less than one year) obliga-

The sharp climb in short-term interest rates pushed Treasury-bill futures quotes up significantly in the summer of 1979. Priced in points of 100 percent. (Chart by Clayton Brokerage Co. of St. Louis)

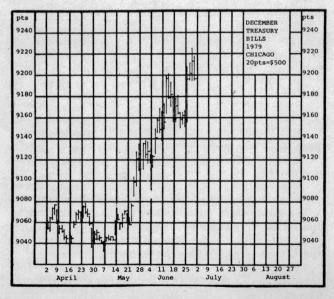

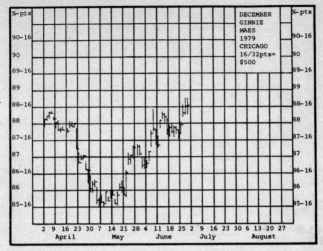

Ginnie Mae futures are fast becoming a big favorite of many investors, and their price performance in 1979 is one of the reasons. Price in 32nds of 100 percent. (Chart by Clayton Brokerage Co. of St. Louis)

tion; Treasury notes, which are intermediate term (one to seven years); and Treasury bonds, which are long-term (over seven years).

In addition, contracts also are traded on, or at least contracts have been proposed on, Government National Mortgage Association (Ginnie Mae) mortgage pass-through certificates, commercial paper (short-term obligations of large United States corporations), and certificates of deposit (large domestic bank CDs maturing in 90 to 180 days).

Simply put, the interest-rate futures game is an investment medium that should be trod only by those investors with a great deal of sophistication. Margin requirements in this sector are extremely small ($1 million of T-bills for $500 initial margin, for instance) and the chance of a quick loss is very high. Caution is the word.

SOME MORE FACTS ABOUT INTEREST-RATE FUTURES: The United States Treasury and the Federal Reserve after viewing the phenomenal growth of financial futures in early 1978 openly admitted that these markets might be so fast and volatile that the government's ability to sell debt and raise needed cash might be impaired. For one thing, they said, interest-rate movements in the futures market caused by the rapid buying and selling might, in fact, result in the government having to pay higher-than-normal interest rates to sell debt. After an extensive study, however, it was determined that the futures markets for these instruments probably do not affect the spot market.

The Interest Rate Markets

Exchange	Size of Contract	Minimum Price Fluctuation	Daily Limit Price Fluctuations
Chicago Board of Trade (Government National Mortgage Assn.)	$100,000	1/32 point or $31.25 per contract	24/32 point ($750 per contract) compared with the previous session's close
(Commercial paper)	$1,000,000	1 point or $25 per contract	25 basis points ($625 per contract) compared with the previous session's close
(Treasury bonds)	$100,000	1/32 point or $31.25 per contract	1 point ($1,000 per contract) compared with the previous session's close
(Treasury notes)	$100,000	1/32 point or $31.25 per contract	16/32 point ($500 per contract) compared with the previous session's close

Exchange	Size of Contract	Minimum Price Fluctuation	Daily Limit Price Fluctuations
Amex Commodities Exchange (Government National Mortgage Assn.) (Treasury bonds)*	$100,000	1/32 point or $31.25 per contract	24/32 point ($750 per contract) compared with the previous session's close
(Treasury notes)*			
(Certificates of Deposit)*	$1,000,000		
Commodity Exchange Inc. (Government National Mortgage Assn.)*			
(Treasury bills)*			
(Treasury notes)*			
Chicago Mercantile Exchange (Treasury bills)	$1,000,000	1 point or $25 per contract	50 points ($1,250 per contract) compared with the previous session's close
MidAmerica Commodity Exchange (Treasury bills)*	$500,000	1 point or $12.50 per contract	50 points ($625 per contract) compared with the previous session's close

Exchange	Size of Contract	Minimum Price Fluctuation	Daily Limit Price Fluctuations
New York Futures Exchange (Treasury bills)*			
(Treasury bonds)*			

* Proposed

PERIODIC REPORTS ON FINANCIAL FUTURES

Bankers' Research, Westport, Conn. (biweekly)
Euromoney, London, England (monthly)
Mortgage Banker, Washington, D.C. (monthly)

The Various Exchanges

An intelligent participant in the futures market takes the time to learn both the strong points and the weak points of the various commodities in which he plans to invest. By the same token, investors also should become acquainted with the strengths and weaknesses of the various exchanges dealing in commodity futures. Indeed, many rules and regulations, even on the same commodity, differ from exchange to exchange. Therefore, research the exchange, its rules, its officers, its committees, and its surveillance operations so that you can become more fully informed on what the world of futures is all about.

AMEX COMMODITIES EXCHANGE

BACKGROUND: Founded in 1978, the Amex Commodities Exchange (ACE) is a result of the startling growth that financial instrument futures have enjoyed in this country over the past few years. Indeed, it was that growth that inspired the American Stock Exchange, the nation's second-largest equities market, to start up ACE as a way to broaden its horizons.

PRODUCTS: The ACE, in line with the Amex's intentions when it started the mart, is solely an exchange dealing in financial-instrument futures. While the exchange currently trades contracts in only Government National Mortgage Association (Ginnie Mae) and ninety-day Treasury bill futures, it has applied to the Commodity Futures Trading Commission for contracts in several additional vehicles, including five-to-seven-year U.S. Treasury notes, long-term U.S. Treasury bonds, domestic certificates of deposit, British pounds, Japanese yen, West German marks, and Swiss francs.

1978 VOLUME: 16,671 contracts traded.

ADDRESS: 86 Trinity Place
New York, NY 10006
(212) 938-6000 (Executive Offices)
(212) 938-2507 (Trading Floor)

OFFICERS: Nathan Most, President
L. A. Blau, Vice President
G. S. Korb, Vice President
A. J. Patti, Vice President

KANSAS CITY BOARD OF TRADE

BACKGROUND: The Kansas City Board of Trade (KCBOT) is a grain exchange that was first organized in 1856 and which today ranks as the nation's eighth-largest futures market.

PRODUCTS: The exchange primarily trades Hard Red Winter Wheat, although it also has approval for a contract on milo, an early growing grain sorghum. Yet, it, too, is branching out because of the lure of financial instrument futures. The exchange has applied to the Commodity Futures Trading Commission to trade a contract that would be based on a stock index, the Value Line Composite Index of 1600 stocks.

1978 VOLUME: 755,949 contracts traded.

ADDRESS: 4800 Main Street, Suite 274
　　　　　Kansas City, MO 64112
　　　　　(816) 753-7363 (Executive Offices)
　　　　　(816) 753-7802 (Public Affairs)
　　　　　(816) 753-7800 (Trading Floor)

OFFICERS: Ira Elsham, President
　　　　　H. R. Schmid, First Vice President
　　　　　W. N. Johnson, Second Vice President
　　　　　W. N. Vernon III, Executive Vice President and Secretary
　　　　　E. D. Romain, Treasurer
　　　　　J. H. Johnson, Comptroller
　　　　　Roderick Turnbull, Director of Public Affairs

CHICAGO BOARD OF TRADE

BACKGROUND: The nation's largest and oldest futures exchange, the Chicago Board of Trade was founded in 1848. In addition, the young listed stock options industry also was spawned within the walls of the CBOT, when in 1973 a group of young CBOT traders started up the Chicago Board Options Exchange (CBOE), which today ranks as the nation's largest options market.

In addition to being a pioneer in the early formation of the futures industry, the CBOT also has emerged as an aggressive leader in promoting and advancing the causes of the present-day futures markets. In 1978, for instance, the CBOT set up a Washington office to improve communications between futures industry officials and the federal government. The exchange also has increased the number of "educational" conferences it sponsors to "get the message out" about the fast-growing markets.

PRODUCTS: The CBOT lists a wide variety of agricultural futures, including wheat, corn, oats, soybeans, soybean oil, soybean meal, iced broilers, and plywood. It also has been moving aggressively into the financial futures area, currently listing contracts in gold, silver, Government National Mortgage Association (Ginnie Mae) bonds, long-term U.S. Treasury bonds, and ninety-day commercial paper.

1978 VOLUME: 27,362,929 contracts traded.

ADDRESS: 141 West Jackson Boulevard
Chicago, IL 60604
(312) 435-3500

OFFICERS: Robert K. Wilmouth, President
Ralph N. Peters, Chairman
Leslie Rosenthal, Vice Chairman
Warren W. Lebeck, Senior Executive Vice President
Paul D. Johns, Vice President, Market and Product Development
Dr. Lloyd Besant, Director of Education

CHICAGO MERCANTILE EXCHANGE

BACKGROUND: The nation's second-largest futures exchange, the Chicago Mercantile Exchange (CME), can be said to be the nation's most aggressive and innovative futures mart. Formed as the Chicago Produce Exchange in 1874, the Chicago Merc originally was a market primarily for perishable agricultural products such as butter, eggs, and poultry. Yet, since it adopted its present name in 1919, the exchange has been a dynamic force of change in the industry. In 1972, for example, it set up a division, the International Monetary Market, which was geared toward trading financial instrument futures. And following that it established another division, the Associate Mercantile Market, to expand some of its agricultural listings.

PRODUCTS: The Chicago Merc's wide menu of contracts makes it the world's largest futures exchange for live commodities, foreign currencies, and U.S. Treasury bills. In the financial instrument area, its IMM division currently lists contracts in eight foreign currencies: West German marks, Canadian dollars, French francs, Swiss francs, Dutch guilders, British pounds, Mexican pesos, and Japanese yen. Included among its product array are copper, gold, U.S. silver coins, and two varieties of U.S. Treasury bills. In the "soft commodity" area, the Chicago Merc has contracts in boneless beef, butter, feeder and live cattle, fresh and frozen eggs, skinned hams, live hogs, lumber, milo, pork bellies, potatoes, and turkeys.

1978 VOLUME: 15,153,952 contracts traded.

ADDRESS: 444 West Jackson Boulevard
      Chicago, IL 60606
      (312) 648-1000

OFFICERS: Clayton K. Yeutter, President
      Beverly J. Spane, Executive Vice President
      Ronald J. Frost, Vice President, Public Information and Marketing
      Glenn R. Windstrup, Vice President, Operations
      Michael D. Weiner, Vice President, Law and Compliance

COMMODITY EXCHANGE INC.

BACKGROUND: The highly profitable Commodity Exchange Inc. of New York, known as the Comex, is the nation's third-largest futures exchange and the world's largest metals futures exchange. It was formed in 1933 by the merger of four other futures exchanges that had been making markets in metals, as well as hides, raw silk, and rubber. The Comex is a very successful exchange and constantly is the object of rumors that have it merging with other futures exchanges. In fact, at the time of this writing, the Comex was discussing a possible merger with the New York Mercantile Exchange.

PRODUCTS: The exchange's markets in rubber and hides were suspended in 1970 and trading in mercury was stopped in 1975. It currently lists contracts in copper, gold, silver, and zinc.

1978 VOLUME: 8, 973,828 contracts traded.

ADDRESS: Four World Trade Center
New York, NY 10048
(212) 938-2900

OFFICERS: Lowell A. Mintz, Chairman
Lee H. Berendt, President
Frank E. Conti, Vice President, Finance

MIDAMERICA COMMODITY EXCHANGE

BACKGROUND: Founded in 1868, and incorporated as the Chicago Open Board of Trade in 1880, the MidAmerica Commodity Exchange adopted its present name in 1972. Today the MidAmerica ranks as the nation's fourth-largest futures market.

PRODUCTS: The MidAmerica stands apart from its competitors in the futures industry because of the way its contracts are structured as "mini-contracts." Indeed, the MidAmerica's contracts are for much smaller dollar amounts than are contracts on other exchanges, and thus are geared more to appeal to smaller, less wealthy investors. The exchange currently lists the following contracts: live cattle (contract size 20,000 pounds compared with 40,000 pounds on the Chicago Board of Trade); corn (1,000 bushels vs. 5,000 bushels); gold (33.2 troy ounces compared with about 100 troy ounces); hogs (15,000 pounds compared with 30,000 pounds); oats (5,000 bushels, the same); silver bullion (1,000 troy ounces compared with 5,000 troy ounces); soybeans (1,000 bushels compared with 5,000 bushels); and wheat (1,000 bushels compared with 5,000 bushels).

1978 VOLUME: 2,121,189 contracts traded.

ADDRESS: 175 West Jackson Boulevard
Chicago, IL 60604

OFFICERS: Walter Franiak, Chairman
David H. Morgan, President
Mary Ann Andersen, Secretary
Gail Osten, Director of Marketing and Public Relations

MINNEAPOLIS GRAIN EXCHANGE

BACKGROUND: The Minneapolis Grain Exchange was founded in 1881. In terms of current futures volume, the exchange ranks ninth in the United States. However, the Minneapolis Grain Exchange primarily is a cash grain market, and as such, ranks as the largest in the world.

PRODUCTS: Currently, the exchange lists contracts in three futures: oats, Durum wheat, and Spring wheat.

1978 VOLUME: 284,313 contracts traded.

ADDRESS: 400 South Fourth Street
Minneapolis, MN 55415
(612) 338-6212

OFFICERS: Merlin W. Mills, President
John P. Case, Vice President
Ralph V. Hayenga, Second Vice President
Alvin W. Donohoo, Executive Vice President
and Secretary

NEW YORK COCOA EXCHANGE

BACKGROUND: Formed in 1925 after a price collapse caused massive losses for many investors speculating in the cocoa-bean market, the New York Cocoa Exchange now is one of the world's largest futures exchanges for cocoa. At the time of this writing, the exchange, which ranks tenth in the United States, had entered into an agreement to merge with the New York Coffee & Sugar Exchange.

PRODUCTS: In 1975 the exchange inaugurated trading in rubber futures to complement its existing contracts in cocoa.

1978 VOLUME: 222,732 contracts traded.

ADDRESS: 127 John Street
New York, NY 10038
(212) 422-5985

OFFICERS: Jerome M. Spielman, Chairman
Willem Kooyker, Vice Chairman
Walter L. Perkins, President
Paul S. Unger, Secretary and Treasurer

NEW YORK COFFEE & SUGAR EXCHANGE

BACKGROUND: The nation's fifth-largest futures market, the New York Coffee & Sugar Exchange was founded in

1882, when it was known only as the New York Coffee Exchange. Its creation was brought about because of a collapse in the coffee market after a huge supply buildup. In 1914 trading in sugar futures was adopted and in 1916 the name was changed to its present form. Today the exchange is the leading marketplace for futures trading in each of those two commodities. At the time of this writing, the exchange had agreed to a merger with the New York Cocoa Exchange.

PRODUCTS: The exchange currently lists contracts in two grades of coffee and two grades of sugar.

1978 VOLUME: 1,202,607 contracts traded.

ADDRESS: Four World Trade Center
New York, NY 10048
(212) 938-2800

OFFICERS: Andrew A. Scholtz, Chairman
John W. Stillwaggon, First Vice Chairman
Joseph L. Fraites, Second Vice Chairman
Bennett J. Corman, President
John M. Schobel, Jr., Vice President
Alan J. Goldenberg, Treasurer

NEW YORK COTTON EXCHANGE

BACKGROUND: Ranked sixth among United States futures exchanges, the New York Cotton Exchange was formed in 1870 by about 100 local cotton merchants. The exchange has grown and expanded rapidly since that time. But because its charter specifies that the exchange can only trade cotton futures, it has had to set up numerous separate corporations to satisfy its expansion needs. In 1971 the Wool Associates was set up and in 1966 the Citrus Associates was established. In 1974 the exchange organized the Petroleum Associates as it expanded further.

PRODUCTS: While cotton is the exchange's primary contract, its Citrus Associates unit offers contracts in frozen concentrated orange juice, the Wool Associates arm offers contracts in old and new wool, and the Petroleum Associates division offers contracts both in crude oil and liquefied propane.

1978 VOLUME: 1,441,209 contracts traded.

ADDRESS: Four World Trade Center
         New York, NY 10048
         (212) 938-2650
OFFICERS: J. William Donaghy, President

NEW YORK MERCANTILE EXCHANGE

BACKGROUND: The New York Mercantile Exchange, the seventh-largest futures mart in the country, was founded in 1872 as a market for cheese, butter, and eggs. In 1882 it adopted its present name. At the time of this writing, the firm was discussing a merger with the Commodity Exchange Inc. of New York.

PRODUCTS: The New York Merc offers a wide variety of products, comprising both agricultural and financial futures. In the financial area, the exchange lists contracts on the following foreign currencies: West German marks, Canadian dollars, Swiss francs, British pounds, and Japanese yen. It also has two varieties of gold contracts as well as futures contracts in United States silver coins. Other contracts include imported lean beef, palladium, platinum, potatoes, and heating and industrial fuel oil.

1978 VOLUME: 926,793 contracts traded.

ADDRESS: Four World Trade Center
         New York, NY 10048
         (212) 938-2222
OFFICERS: Michel Marks, Chairman
          Dennis Suskind, First Vice Chairman
          Salvatore Calcaterra, Secretary
          C. Victor Buccellato, Treasurer
          Howard Gabler, Executive Vice President

NEW YORK FUTURES EXCHANGE

BACKGROUND: The New York Futures Exchange (NYFE) is a subsidiary of the New York Stock Exchange, the world's largest securities market, and was scheduled to begin trading financial instrument futures in 1980.

PRODUCTS: The NYFE has applied to the Commodity Futures Trading Commission to list contracts in ninety-day Treasury bills, twenty-year Treasury bonds, and five major foreign currencies.

ADDRESS: 11 Wall Street
         New York, NY 10005
         (212) 623-2065
OFFICERS: John J. Phelan, Jr., Chairman
         William M. Smith, President
         Dr. Frank J. Jones, Senior Vice President and
             Director of Economic Research
         Jean M. Blin, Senior Vice President
         Agnes Gautier, Vice President, Regulation and
             Surveillance

What Is the Function of the Clearinghouse?

One of the most important, but least publicized, aspects of the futures markets is the role of the clearinghouses which serve the various exchanges. Indeed, in 1978 the clearinghouses serving this nation's futures exchanges handled futures transactions that involved an aggregate of $1.4 trillion of investors' money. In doing so, these bodies saw to it that contracts either were settled, offset, or fulfilled. It is a task that makes the markets as sound and as orderly as they are. But that was not always the case.

In fact, when the United States' futures markets were still in their infant stages prior to 1900 futures transactions not only were entered into face-to-face by the principals involved, but those principals also generally had to meet later to settle the transaction. That is, they generally had to decide how and when to deliver the physical commodities or if both parties agreed to cancel the arrangement.

But as the markets grew busier and more complex it soon became evident that a better system would be needed. Indeed, many of the farmers and commercial firms who were becoming increasingly involved in the markets were beginning to learn that instead of subjecting themselves to the vagaries of the marketplace and thus having to deliver or buy the crops they could effectively hedge their positions by assuming opposite positions in the market. This development made the need for a clearing arm all the more necessary because the settlements generally were more in the area of deciding how positions were to be offset than in determining how a crop actually should be delivered.

As a result, the age-old practice of buyers and sellers meeting to settle their contracts no longer was feasible. This settlement function, instead, became the task of clerks at the various brokerage houses. They, in turn, would keep track of the various buyers and sellers of contracts so that when the expiration date finally did arrive, there would not be any question as to who owned the contract and what that person's responsibilities were.

In the 1920s, however, the settlement function took another step, as many of the nation's formal futures exchanges began to set up their own clearing operations. Indeed, the clearinghouses took on very important tasks. The Chicago Board of Trade's Commodity Trading Manual sums it up best: "Regardless of corporate structure, clearinghouses and clearing corporations act as third parties to all futures contracts—acting as buyer to every seller and seller to every buyer."

For example, buyers and sellers of futures contracts do not actually enter into financial transactions with each other in today's futures markets. Instead, the buyer agrees to buy through the clearinghouse and the seller agrees to sell through the clearinghouse. By setting up the market in such a way, safeguards are built into the system and they, in turn, protect every investor, whether small speculator or large commercial firm, coming into the market.

VI. The Futures Market: Databank

To complete your education in trading futures contracts and so this book can serve as a handy reference guide for you, the following information is provided.

SAMPLE COMMISSION RATES

	Regular Trade	Spread Trade
Chicago Board of Trade		
Broilers	$50.50	$66.00
Commercial Paper	61.00	82.00
Corn	40.50	53.00
GNMA	61.00	82.00
Gold	50.50	66.00
Soybean Meal	50.50	66.00
Oats	40.50	53.00
Soybean Oil	50.50	66.00
Plywood	50.50	66.00
Silver	50.50	66.00
Soybeans	50.50	66.00
Treasury Bonds	61.00	82.00
Wheat	50.50	66.00
Chicago Mercantile Exchange		
Boneless Beef	51.50	68.00
Butter	51.50	68.00
Eggs	51.50	68.00
Feeder Cattle	51.50	68.00

	Regular Trade	Spread Trade
Hams	51.50	68.00
Live Cattle	51.50	68.00
Live Hogs	51.50	68.00
Lumber	51.50	68.00
Milo	51.50	68.00
Pork Bellies	51.50	68.00
Russet Potatoes	76.50	97.50
British Pounds	51.50	68.00
Canadian Dollars	51.50	68.00
Canadian Silver Coins	51.50	68.00
Copper	51.50	68.00
Dutch Guilders	51.50	68.00
West German Marks	51.50	68.00
French Francs	51.50	68.00
Gold	51.50	68.00
Japanese Yen	51.50	68.00
Mexican Pesos	51.50	68.00
Swiss Francs	51.50	68.00
Treasury Bills	61.50	83.00
U.S. Silver Coins	51.50	68.00
New York exchanges		
Boneless Beef	50.00	65.00
Cocoa	75.00	98.00
Coffee	80.00 to 90.00	96.00 to 108.00
Copper	51.50	68.00
Cotton	60.00 to 77.00	92.50 to 110.50
Frozen Orange Juice	52.00	69.00
Gold	51.50	68.00
Palladium	50.00 to 75.00	65.00 to 97.50
Platinum	50.00	65.00
Propane	50.00	65.00
Round White Potatoes	50.00	65.00
Silver	51.50	68.00
Silver Coins	50.00	65.00
Sugar	50.00 to 75.00	65.00 to 97.50

SAMPLE MARGINS

	Minimum Margins	
	Initial	Maintenance
Chicago Board of Trade		
Iced Broilers	$500	$400
Commercial Paper	750	600
Corn	600	400
GNMA	1,000	750
Gold	1,200	900
Oats	400	250

	Minimum Margins	
	Initial	**Maintenance**
Plywood	700	400
Silver	1,500	1,000
Soybeans	3,000	2,000
Soybean Meal	1,200	750
Soybean Oil	1,250	900
Treasury Bonds	1,250	1,000
Wheat	1,000	600
Chicago Mercantile Exchange		
Boneless Beef	900	700
Butter	750	450
Feeder Cattle	1,500	1,200
Live Cattle	1,200	900
Shell Eggs	700	500
Frozen Eggs	600	400
Ham	1,000	700
Stud Lumber	800	500
Milo	400	300
Pork Bellies	1,500	1,000
Russet Potatoes	500	350
Copper	500	350
West German Marks	2,000	1,500
Canadian Dollar	1,500	1,000
French Franc	1,500	1,000
Swiss Franc	3,000	2,000
Dutch Guilder	1,500	1,000
British Pound	1,500	1,000
Mexican Peso	2,500	2,000
Japanese Yen	2,000	1,500
U.S. Silver Coins	750	600
Treasury Bill	600 to 800	400 to 600
New York exchanges		
GNMA	1,000	750
Copper	1,000	750
Gold	1,000	750
Silver	2,000	1,500
Zinc	750	562.50
Cocoa	2,000	1,500
Rubber	750	562.50
Coffee	4,500	2,250
Sugar	1,000 to 1,300	500 to 650
Cotton	1,000	750
Orange Juice	1,500	1,125
Palladium	800	560
Platinum	1,500	1,050
U.S. Silver Coins	1,500	1,050

POOL OPERATORS

Arnomax Corporation
2131 The Alameda
San Jose, CA 95126
(408) 984-3327

David R. Aronson
505 Park Avenue, 21st Floor
New York, NY 10022
(212) 371-0109
(212) 725-2087

Bengal Investment Corp.
1556 E. Commercial Boulevard
Ft. Lauderdale, FL 33334
(305) 776-6380

Bluewater Commodity Services
P.O. Box 6418
Lake Charles, LA 70606

Blyth Eastman Dillon
1221 Avenue of the Americas,
    14th floor
New York, NY 10020
(212) 730-6312

Carroll Commodities
2332 Sykesville Road
Westminster, MD 21157
(301) 876-1552

Church of Gospel Ministry,
    Inc.
228 Cooper Street
Camden, NJ 08102

CLP Management, Inc.
175 W. Jackson Boulevard
    Suite 1440
Chicago, IL 60604
(312) 922-5645

Commodity Investments Inter-
    national
5368 Brockbank Place
San Diego, CA 92115
(714) 286-2942

Commodity Specialists, Inc.
1515 S. Rock Hill Road
St. Louis, MO 63119
(314) 962-8832

Commodity Systems, Inc.
150 E. Palmetto Park Road,
    Suite 515
Boca Raton, FL 33432
(305) 392-8663

Robert H. Conner
141 W. Jackson Boulevard,
    Suite 2750
Chicago, IL 60604
(312) 987-9845

Conservative Commodities
    Corp.
521 Wall Street, Suite 312
P.O. Box 21294
Seattle, WA 98111
(206) 682-7903

ContiCommodity
1800 Board of Trade Building
Chicago, IL 60604
(312) 786-0800

C.R.A.M.I.T. Associated
335 East Carter Drive
Tempe, AZ 85282
(602) 839-2592

Decade Management Company
2120 Main Street, Suite 260
Huntington Beach, CA 92648
(714) 960-6030

Edward T. de Lanoy
50 Chestnut Street
San Carlos, CA 94070
(415) 593-5664

Dunn & Hargitt, Inc.
22 North Second Street
Lafayette, IN 47902
(317) 423-2626

Eastern Management Fund,
  Inc.
One Washington Mall, Suite
  1550
Boston, MA 02108
(800) 225-2482 Toll-free
(617) 542-0505 Collect
  (Mass.)

Endymion Commodities, Inc.
131 State Street, Suite 616
Boston, MA 02109
(617) 367-9690

Fairfax Management Co.
141 W. Jackson Boulevard,
  Suite 1800
Chicago, IL 60604
(312) 786-0800

First Guaranty Metals Co. Inc.
1000 Brickell Avenue
Miami, FL 33131
(305) 358-3666
(800) 327-2411

Fraenkel & Company
750 North 115th Street
Wahwatosa, WI 53226
(414) 771-3344

Funded Equities Inc.
140 Cedar Street, Suite 616
New York, NY 10006
(212) 233-6000

John Gabriel Corp.
340 East 86th Street
New York, NY 10028
(212) 288-1119

GLC Advisors, Ltd.
211 C Street
Silverton, OR 97381
(503) 873-5808

Global Commodities Inc.
999 Brickell Avenue #530
Miami, FL 33131
(305) 379-9999

Gary Goodman
1380 Midvale
Los Angeles, CA 90024
(213) 478-6649

The Grain Observer
P.O. Box 7
Matteson, IL 60443
(312) 748-1782

Heinold Commodities, Inc.
222 S. Riverside Plaza
Chicago, IL 61434
(312) 648-8000

Investment Survival
1002 N.W. Bond Street
Bend, OR 97701
(503) 382-8449

Investors' Commodities Corp.
115 Broadway
New York, NY 10006
(212) 285-0273

Investors Commodity Manual,
  Ltd.
1112 First National Bank
  Building
Tampa, FL 33602
(813) 223-1181
(813) 224-0161

Michael R. Kay
Archer Commodities, Inc.
175 W. Jackson Boulevard
Chicago, IL 60604
(312) 427-6311

LVM Commodities
2425 Torreya Drive
Tallahassee, FL 32303
(904) 385-0933

New Orleans Commodity
    Advisors
P.O. Box 50371
New Orleans, LA 70150
(601) 255-2597

Norwood Securities
6134 N. Milwaukee Avenue
Chicago, IL 60646
(312) 763-1540

Pacific Commodity Fund
455 S. Broadway
P.O. Box 756
Estacada, OR 97023
(503) 630-7751

PMA Commodities
133 Federal Street
Boston, MA 02110
(800) 225-2486
(617) 338-2100

Pooled Equity Partners
202 Midland Park Office
    Building
2817 Anthony Lane South
St. Anthony Village, MN 55418

PWA Commodity Research
2607 Partridge Avenue
Arlington, TX 76017
(817) 465-5105

Roy D. Spiegel, C.T.A.
340 East 86th Street
New York, NY 10028
(212) 288-5665

Tara, Inc.
3521 34th Street
Lubbock, TX 79410
(806) 792-6351

Harry R. Thomas Co. Inc.
2900 Kentucky Street, N.E.
Albuquerque, NM 87110
(505) 881-1575

Thomson McKinnon Securities
    Inc.
One New York Plaza
New York, NY 10004
(212) 482-7000

Thomte & Co., Inc.
47 Commercial Wharf
Boston, MA 02110
(617) 523-3505

Western Financial Manage-
    ment
3031 Tisch Way #812
San Jose, CA 95128
(408) 249-1740

Robert F. Wiest
4204 Minnecota
Thousand Oaks, CA 91360
(805) 495-4947

Yorkstone Research Inc.
41 State Street
Albany, NY 12207
(518) 463-4423

FIRMS OFFERING MANAGED ACCOUNTS

Accurate Day Trade Services
P.O. Box 682
Somerville, NJ 08876
(201) 526-2645

Ace American, Inc.
TransAmerica Building
600 Montgomery Street, 8th
   Floor
San Francisco, CA 94111
(415) 392-6717

ACLI International Com-
   modity Services, Inc.
717 Westchester Avenue
White Plains, NY 10604
(914) 683-8273

Advanced Market Technology
3544 Lincoln Avenue, Suite 4
Ogden, UT 84403
(801) 621-0860

A.I.M. Services
P.O. Box 607
Lake Havasu City, AZ 86403

Archer Commodities Inc.
175 W. Jackson Boulevard
Chicago, IL 60604
(312) 427-6025
(800) 621-4781

Arnomax Corporation
2131 The Alameda
San Jose, CA 95126
(408) 984-3327

David R. Aronson
505 Park Avenue, 21st Floor
New York, NY 10022
(212) 371-0109
(212) 725-2087

Bayer, Griffin Inc.
19 Virginia Avenue
Rockville Centre, NY 11570
(800) 645-2302 Toll-free
(516) 766-2122

Bengal Investment Corp.
1556 E. Commercial Boulevard
Fort Lauderdale, FL 33334
(305) 776-6380

Bengal Trading Corp.
1556 E. Commercial Boulevard
Fort Lauderdale, FL 33334
(305) 776-6360

Bentley & Co., Ltd.
Atlas House
Hamilton, Bermuda
U.S. Representative:
Bassetti & Co., Ltd.
1413 Kearny
San Francisco, CA 94133
(415) 788-7887

Buell Commodity Co.
1907 B Waters Edge
Fort Collins, CO 80526
(303) 484-5972

C² Inc.
Navy Lane
Essex, CT 06426

Cambridge Commodities Corp.
Kendall Square Building, Suite
   301
Cambridge, MA 02142
(617) 661-6752

Campbell & Company
The Village of Cross Keys
Baltimore, MD 21210
(301) 435-1131

Capital Futures Associates,
   Ltd.
P.O. Box 2618
Chicago, IL 60690
(312) 274-9254

Charter Financial Group
3000 Post Oak Road, Suite
   1480
Houston, TX 77056
(713) 621-1681

The Chartist
30 W. Washington Street,
   Suite 1432
Chicago, IL 60602
(312) 641-1109

Chicago Futures Analysts, Inc.
175 W. Jackson Boulevard,
   Room A1416
Chicago, IL 60604
(312) 786-0192

Cibola Investment Consultants,
   Inc.
664 Main Street
Amherst, MA 01002
(413) 253-2808

CISCOM, Inc.
4232 Brandywine Drive
P.O. Box 3878
Peoria, IL 61614
(309) 692-0630

Norris L. Clark & Associates,
   Inc.
2100 Park Street
Syracuse, NY 13208
(315) 472-7514

Clayton Brokerage Co. of St.
   Louis, Inc.
7701 Forsyth Boulevard,
   Suite 300
St. Louis, MO 63105
(314) 727-8000

CLP Management, Inc.
175 W. Jackson Boulevard,
   Suite 1440
Chicago, IL 60604
(312) 922-5645

Cohn Commodities, Inc.
39 Church Street
P.O. Box 2083
New Haven, CT 06521
(203) 789-0060

Combined Investor Services,
   Inc.
215 Heritage National Bank
   Building
Tyler, TX 75703
(214) 561-9600

Comm Basic Inc. Associates
7920 Chambersburg Road
Dayton, OH 45424
(513) 233-9904

Commodity Investment Ser-
   vice, Inc.
20370 Town Center Lane,
   Suite 250
Cupertino, CA 95014
(408) 446-1212

Commodity Management Ser-
   vice Corp.
33 W. Ridge Pike
Limerick, PA 19468
(215) 489-4188

Commodity Managers Group
1575 Dutton Road
Rochester, MI 48063
(313) 652-4770

Commodity Microanalysis Inc.
4106 Loch Haven Boulevard
Baltimore, MD 21218
(301) 366-8200

Commodity Research Institute
Box 1866
Hendersonville, NC 28739
(704) 692-6971

Commodity Specialists, Inc.
1515 S. Rock Hill Road
St. Louis, MO 63119
(314) 962-8832

Commodity Systems, Inc.
150 E. Palmetto Park Road,
  Suite 515
Boca Raton, FL 33432
(305) 392-8663

Commodity Timing
850 Munras Avenue, Suite
  Two
Monterey, CA 93940
(408) 372-1800

Commodity Trend Service
100 E. Kimberly Road
Northwest Tower, Suite 303
Davenport, IA 52808
(319) 386-2950

Comtek Commodities Co.
130 Los Aguajes Avenue
Santa Barbara, CA 93101
(805) 962-0109

Dale E. Comyford
P.O. Box 8972
Denver, CO 80201
(303) 779-5202

Robert H. Conner
141 W. Jackson Boulevard,
  Suite 2750
Chicago, IL 60604
(312) 987-9845

Continental Resources
1180 Reed Avenue, #52
Sunnyvale, CA 94086
(408) 249-8235

C.R.A.M.I.T. Associated
335 East Carter Drive
Tempe, AZ 85282
(602) 839-2592

Cycle System Index, Inc.
P.O. Box 271
Berne, IN 46711
(219) 589-2678

Morgan J. Daley Corp.
974 Paul Brown Building
St. Louis, MO 63101
(314) 621-2078

Decade Management Company
2120 Main Street, Suite 260
Huntington Beach, CA 92648
(714) 960-6030

Delta Financial Research, Inc.
1724 Sherman Avenue
Evanston, IL 60201
(312) 491-1130

Desai & Company
437 Lytton Avenue, Suite 200
Palo Alto, CA 94301
(415) 327-4364

Dunn & Hargitt, Inc.
22 North Second Street
Lafayette, IN 47902
(317) 423-2626

Eastern Management Fund,
  Inc.
One Washington Mall, Suite
  1550
Boston, MA 02108
(800) 225-2482 Toll-free
(617) 542-0505 Collect
  (Mass.)

Eilen Commodities, Ltd.
99-32 66th Road
Rego Park, NY 11374
(212) 830-0267
910-221-1122 Telex

Equity Guarantee and Man-
agement
6445 12th Avenue, South
Minneapolis, MN 55423
(612) 633-7894

Financial Investment Tech-
nalysis Corp.
P.O. Box 6121
San Mateo, CA 94403
(415) 348-2666

First Commodity Corporation
of Boston
19 Congress Street
Boston, MA 02109
(617) 523-1138

First Continental Commodities
Inc.
309 Grain Exchange Building
Winnipeg, Manitoba R3B OT6
(204) 944-0714

First Guaranty Metals Co., Inc.
1000 Brickell Avenue
Miami, FL 33131
(305) 358-3666
(800) 327-2411

Robert A. Forman, CTA
2131 The Alameda
San Jose, CA 95126
(408) 984-3327

Fraenkel & Company
750 North 115th Street
Wahwatosa, WI 53226
(414) 771-3344

Funded Equities Inc.
140 Cedar Street, Suite 616
New York, NY 10006
(212) 233-6000

Futurecom Management, Inc.
3450 West Central Avenue,
Suite 101
Toledo, OH 43606
(419) 535-7945

Futures Equity Management,
Inc.
601 N. Rowell Avenue
Manhattan Beach, CA 90266
(213) 379-5923

Futures Management Co.
591 Camino de la Reina,
#1026
San Diego, CA 92108
(714) 299-7932

Futures Management Corp. of
Iowa
100 Westpark Plaza
RR #3
Clear Lake, IA 50428
(515) 357-6555

John Gabriel Corp.
340 East 86th Street
New York, NY 10028
(212) 288-1119

GLC Advisors, Ltd.
211 C Street
Silverton, OR 97381
(503) 873-5808

Commodity Cycles
P.O. Box 40070
Tucson, AZ 85717
(602) 884-5947

Harbor Investments, Inc.
Bay 214 Union Wharf
Boston, MA 02109
(617) 523-0620

Len Harrison
141 W. Jackson Boulevard,
  Suite 1025
Chicago, IL 60604
(312) 786-0900 Ext. 256

William Hemphill
437 Lytton Avenue
Palo Alto, CA 94301
(415) 328-7374

Heritage Commodity Con-
  sultants, Inc.
375 Distel Circle, Suite D-8
Los Altos, CA 94022
(415) 964-6633

Hogan-Orr, Commodity
  Specialist
175 W. Jackson, A917
Chicago, IL 60604
(312) 663-0350

The House of Insight
Box 1412
Portland, OR 97207
(503) 226-1631

Incomco Inc.
1 World Trade Center
New York, NY 10048
(212) 466-1350
(800) 221-4380

International Futures Management Corp.
5100 Westheimer, Suite 200
Houston, TX 77056
(713) 627-0541

Investment Survival
1002 N.W. Bond Street
Bend, OR 97701
(503) 382-8449

January Management Asso-
  ciates
165 East 33rd Street
New York, NY 10016
(212) 532-4825

Michael R. Kay
Archer Commodities, Inc.
175 W. Jackson Boulevard
Chicago, IL 60604
(312) 427-6311

LeCompte's Managed Ac-
  counts
406 S. Lincoln
Urbana, IL 61801
(217) 367-2001

Lewis Research Associates,
  Inc.
P.O. Box 52
Mendenhall, PA 19357

LTZ Management Corpora-
  tion
175 W. Jackson Boulevard,
  Room A235
Chicago, IL 60604
(800) 621-4753 Toll-free
(312) 427-6070 Ill. only

LVM Commodities
2425 Torreya Drive
Tallahassee, FL 32303
(904) 385-0933

David K. MacQuown
P.O. Box 541
Carmel, CA 93921

Managed Accounts Reports
224 Joseph Square
Columbia, MD 21044
(301) 730-5365

Managed Commodity Trading
  Accounts
Box 3117 Bahia Mar
Fort Lauderdale, FL 33316
(305) 463-0438

MBH Commodity Advisors
P.O. Box 353
Winnetka, IL 60093
(312) 398-4620

MGC Commodity Corp.
666 Fifth Avenue
New York, NY 10019
(212) 581-2400

Mid Am Advisory Service
1157 W. Farwell Avenue
Chicago, IL 60626
(312) 338-8236

Murlas Brothers Commodities
5450 W. Fullerton Avenue
Chicago, IL 60639
(800) 621-1008

Neuberger Securities Corp.
111 Broadway
New York, NY 10006
(212) 766-1700

New Orleans Commodity
  Advisors
P.O. Box 50371
New Orleans, LA 70150
(601) 255-2597

Norwood Securities
6134 N. Milwaukee Avenue
Chicago, IL 60646
(312) 763-1540

Ohio Commodity Corp.
P.O. Box 29531
Columbus, OH 43229
(614) 890-8881

Options Market, Inc.
270 Spring Valley Road
Paramus, NJ 07652
(201) 262-0353

Pacific Commodity Fund
455 S. Broadway
P.O. Box 756
Estacada, OR 97023
(503) 630-7751

Walter B. Parker
1165 Empire Central Place,
  Suite 115
Dallas, TX 75247
(214) 630-0403

PMA Commodities
133 Federal Street
Boston, MA 02110
(800) 225-2486
(617) 338-2100

PWA Commodity Research
2607 Partridge Avenue
Arlington, TX 76017
(817) 465-5150

Quantitative Trading Strategies
1213 Lincoln Avenue, Suite
  100
San Jose, CA 95125
(408) 293-0739

John A. Quimby Associates,
  Inc.
80 Rogers Street, Suite 8D
Clearwater, FL 33516
(813) 443-3449

Raymond, James & Associates,
  Inc.
6090 Central Avenue
St. Petersburg, FL 33707
(813) 381-3800

Rende Management
c/o Bache Halsey Stuart
    Shields, Inc.
350 California Street
San Francisco, CA 94104
(415) 981-0440

R. Rowland and Co., Inc.
100 North Broadway
St. Louis, MO 63102
(314) 342-2800

San Miguel Associates
P.O. Box 610
Point Reyes, CA 94956
(415) 663-8321

SCT/Systems Commodity
    Trading
1413 Kearny Street
San Francisco, CA 94133
(415) 788-7887

The Siegel Trading Co., Inc.
4205 Hillsboro Road
Hobbs Building, Suite 204
Nashville, TN 37215
(615) 385-3490

Roy D. Spiegel, C.T.A.
340 East 86th Street
New York, NY 10028
(212) 288-5665

Nicholas Suzick
6340 La Jolla Boulevard
La Jolla, CA 92037
(714) 454-9895

SAM/System Advisors Mar-
    keting
1413 Kearny
San Francisco, CA 94133
(415) 788-7887

TARA, Inc.
3521 34th Street
Lubbock, TX 79410
(806) 792-6351

Harry R. Thomas Co., Inc.
2900 Kentucky Street, N.E.
Albuquerque, NM 87110
(505) 881-1575

Thomte & Co., Inc.
47 Commercial Wharf
Boston, MA 02110
(617) 523-3505

The Timing Index
P.O. Box 1637
Studio City, CA 91604
(213) 654-1401

Tradefix Co.
P.O. Box 273
Church Street Station
New York, NY 10007
(212) 639-5503

Trendview Management
P.O. Box 80592
San Diego, CA 92138
(714) 231-1708

Western Financial Manage-
    ment
3031 Tisch Way #812
San Jose, CA 95128
(408) 249-1740

Robert F. Wiest
4204 Minnecota
Thousand Oaks, CA 91360
(805) 495-4947

Yorkstone Research Inc.
41 State Street
Albany, NY 12207
(518) 463-4423

CHARTING SERVICES

Commodity Information Services
175 West Jackson Boulevard,
  Suite 1021
Chicago, IL 60604
(312) 922-3661

Commodity Perspective
Investor Publishing Inc.
327 South LaSalle
Chicago, IL 60604
(312) 341-1399

Commodity Price Charts
219 Parkade
Cedar Falls, IA 50613
(319) 277-6341

Commodity Research Bureau
  Inc.
1 Liberty Plaza
New York, NY 10006
(212) 267-3600

Commodity Trend Service
100 East Kimberly Road
Northwest Tower, Suite 303
Davenport, IA, 52808
(319) 386-2950

Comtrend Inc.
25 Third Street
Stamford, CT 06905
(203) 357-1611

Data Lab Inc.
200 West Monroe Street,
  No. 1106
Chicago, IL 60606
(312) 236-8162

Doane Agricultural Service
  Inc.
8900 Manchester Road
St. Louis, MO 63144
(314) 968-1000

Dunn & Hargitt Inc.
22 North Second Street
Lafayette, IN 47902
(317) 423-2626

Commodity Cycles
Post Office Box 40070
Tucson, AZ 85717
(602) 884-5947

IBEX Chart Service Inc.
Box 693
2420 First Avenue
Seattle, WA 98121

MJK Associates
122 Saratoga Avenue
Suite 11
Santa Clara, CA 95050
(408) 247-5102

The Professional Chart Service
Hadady Publications
61 South Lake Avenue, Suite
  309R
Pasadena, CA 91101
(213) 681-2789

Remote Computing Corp.
1076 East Meadow Circle
Palo Alto, CA 94303
(415) 494-6111

Ruf Stock and Commodity
  Charts
22 Garfield Place
Poughkeepsie, NY 12601
(914) 452-1876

Security Market Research Inc.
Dept. CM, Post Office Box
  14096
Denver, CO 80214
(303) 422-4231

Spread Scope Inc.
Post Office Box 41221
Los Angeles, CA 90041

Top Farmers of America
225 East Michigan
Milwaukee, WI 53202
(414) 278-7676

Tradecenter Division
CMT Corp.
11 Graphic Place
Moonachie, NJ 07074
(201) 440-4800

Traders Press
Post Office Box 10344
Greenville, SC 29603
(803) 271-9484

SOURCES OF MARKET INFORMATION

Because events in both the futures market and the cash commodity markets often can change so rapidly, supplemental sources of information have been set up to keep investors abreast of market happenings on any particular day. One way this is accomplished is through a network of telephone services in several states which use recorded market synopses, which are updated regularly, to keep the public informed. The lines currently are available for grain, poultry and eggs. Here is the list:

Grain

Arkansas
Carlisle (501) 552-3361
DeWitt (501) 946-2796
Lakevillage (501) 265-2990
Lewisville (501) 921-4742
Little Rock (501) 376-4601 (Ext. 391)
Lonoke (501) 676-6889
Marianna (501) 295-5080
Newport (501) 523-8405
Pine Bluff (501) 535-3170
Stuttgart (501) 673-1736
Walnut Ridge (501) 886-5339
California
Los Angeles (213) 622-7822
Colorado
Denver (303) 837-4786
District of Columbia
Washington (202) 447-8233
Idaho
Pocatello (800) 632-9494 (within state only)

Illinois
  Springfield (217) 782-2055
Indiana
  Indianapolis (800) 382-1567 (within state only)
Iowa
  Des Moines (515) 281-3755
Kansas
  Kansas City (913) 831-2929
Kentucky
  Louisville (502) 584-6617
Louisiana
  Baton Rouge (504) 925-4640
Minnesota
  Minneapolis (612) 725-2652
Mississippi
  Jackson (1-800) 222-7188 (within state only, 4:30 p.m. to
    8:30 a.m.)
Missouri
  Jefferson City (314) 636-4203
Montana
  Great Falls (800) 332-5906 (within state only)
               (800) 332-5909 (within state only)
               (800) 322-5913 (within state only)
               (406) 761-5906 (outside of state)
North Carolina
  Raleigh (919) 829-2147
North Dakota
  Fargo (800) 342-4914 (within state only)
Oklahoma
  Oklahoma City (1-800) 522-8171 (within state only)
                (405) 521-0466
Oregon
  Portland (503) 221-2022
           (503) 221-3426
South Carolina
  Columbia (803) 758-8100
Tennessee
  Jackson (901) 423-2080
  Knoxville (615) 525-3211
  Nashville (800) 342-8206 (within state only)
            (615) 833-4046
Texas
  Amarillo (806) 352-7411
  Austin (512) 475-4287
  Corpus Christi (512) 884-0911
  El Paso (915) 533-1514
  Lubbock (806) 763-3285
  Spur (806) 271-4505

Vernon (817) 552-7541
Virginia
  Onley (804) 787-3500
  Richmond (804) 786-8749
  Warsaw (804) 333-5241
  Windsor (804) 242-6978
Washington
  Spokane (800) 572-5952 (within state only)
Wisconsin
  Madison (608) 266-6760

Livestock

Alabama
  Montgomery (800) 392-5804 (within state only, cattle re-
              ports 5 p.m. to 8 a.m.)
            (800) 392-5801 (within state only, hog reports
              5 p.m. to 8 a.m.)
Arizona
  Phoenix (602) 275-7972
Arkansas
  Fort Smith (501) 785-3892
  Little Rock (501) 372-3933
California
  Bell (213) 268-8020
  El Centro (714) 352-8160
  Reeding (916) 246-8480
  Stockton (209) 466-3085
  Visalia (209) 733-3750
Colorado
  Brush (303) 842-2249
  Greeley (303) 353-5170
  Longmount (303) 776-7820
  Pueblo (303) 948-2407
  Sterling (303) 522-4772
Florida
  Fort Pierce (305) 465-5239
  Winter Park (305) 628-0412
Georgia
  Thomasville (800) 342-1440 (within state only)
Idaho
  Pocatello (800) 632-9494 (within state only)
  Burley (208) 678-2424
Illinois
  Chicago (312) 922-1253
  Joliet (815) 423-5026
  Peoria (309) 676-8811

National Stock Yards (618) 874-1900
Springfield (217) 525-4019
Indiana
Indianapolis (800) 382-1567 (within state only)
Iowa
Ames (515) 294-6899
        (515) 294-4347
Des Moines (515) 282-6870
Durant (319) 785-6032
Sioux City (712) 252-2100
Kansas
Dodge City (316) 225-1311
Wichita (316) 267-7992
Kentucky
Frankfort (502) 564-4958
Louisville (502) 584-6617
Michigan
Lansing (517) 373-6330
Minnesota
South St. Paul (612) 451-3692
Mississippi
Jackson (601) 355-3176
Missouri
Jefferson City (314) 636-4203
Joplin (417) 781-9451
Kansas City (816) 421-7694
Mexico (314) 581-6250 (not available at certain hours)
South St. Joseph (816) 238-1203
Springfield (417) 866-4986
West Plains (417) 256-9631
Montana
Billings (406) 252-1480
Nebraska
Aurora (402) 694-3183
Beatrice (402) 223-5231
Beemer (402) 528-3654
Columbus (402) 564-1133
Exeter (402) 266-5461
Grand Island (308) 384-5101
Kearney (308) 237-5908
Lincoln (402) 477-3238
Omaha (402) 731-5355
Superior (402) 879-4600
Tekamah (402) 374-1667
West Point (402) 372-5650
York (402) 362-6623
New Mexico
Clovis (505) 763-3030

New York
  Albany (518) 457-6672
North Dakota
  West Fargo (701) 282-5493
Ohio
  Chillicothe (614) 772-1431
  Columbus (614) 466-6484
  London (614) 852-2311
  Washington (614) 335-5100
Oklahoma
  Oklahoma City (405) 236-5491
  Tulsa (918) 437-0740
Pennsylvania
  New Holland (717) 354-7288
South Carolina
  Columbia (803) 799-5568
  Walterboro (803) 549-5232
South Dakota
  Rapid City (605) 342-1833
  Sioux Falls (605) 336-7765
Tennessee
  Jackson (901) 423-2080
  Knoxville (615) 525-3211
  Nashville (615) 833-4046
Texas
  Amarillo (806) 372-3494
  Corsicana (214) 872-4001
  Fort Worth (817) 624-7451
  San Angelo (915) 655-2358
  San Antonio (512) 223-4100
  Sealy (713) 885-2050
Utah
  North Salt Lake (801) 524-5001 (5 p.m. to 7:30 a.m.)
  Salina (801) 529-7000
Washington
  Sunnyside (509) 837-2412
West Virginia
  Charleston (304) 348-8883 (2 p.m. to 11 a.m.)
Wisconsin
  Madison (608) 266-9444
Wyoming
  Cheyenne (307) 777-7959
  Torrington (307) 532-7200

Poultry and Eggs

California
  Los Angeles (213) 622-0784

Georgia
   Atlanta (404) 881-3075 (eggs)
         (404) 881-3073 (poultry)
Illinois
   Chicago (312) 922-2030 (eggs)
         (312) 922-2997 (poultry and turkeys)
Louisiana
   Baton Rouge (504) 925-4640
Missouri
   St. Louis (314) 425-6000
New Jersey
   Newark (201) 645-3369 (eggs)
         (201) 621-6619 (poultry)
Oregon
   Portland (503) 221-2350
Texas
   Austin (512) 475-3845

FREE MARKET LITERATURE

To further your knowledge of the futures market, the following literature is available free from the various exchanges:

Chicago Board of Trade, 141 W. Jackson Boulevard, Chicago, IL 60604
   Introduction to Hedging
   Trading in Broiler Futures
   Trading in Corn Futures
   Trading in Plywood Futures
   Trading in Soybean Meal
   Hedging: Plywood Futures
   Action in the Marketplace: Trading Commodity Futures
   Futures Trading for the Performance-Minded Investor
   An Introduction to the Interest Rate Futures Market
   Making and Taking Delivery on Interest Rate Futures Contracts
   Hedging Interest Rate Risks
   A Perspective on Yields
   What in the World is Happening to the Price of Soybeans and Why

Chicago Mercantile Exchange, 444 W. Jackson Boulevard, Chicago, IL 60606
   Banker Hedging
   Commodity Trader's Scorecard
   Livestock Hedger's Workbook

How to Make Livestock Futures Work for You
Trading in Tomorrows
CME Newsletter
Before You Speculate
A Guide to Silver Coin Futures
Trading in Silver Coin Futures
Understanding Futures in Foreign Exchange
Trading in International Currency Futures
Gold Futures: Contract Specifications
Weekly IMM Gold Fundamentals
U.S. Treasury-Bill Contract Specifications (13-week and 1-year)
T-Bill Futures, Opportunities in Interest Rates
Four-Year U.S. Treasury Notes

Commodity Exchange, Inc., 4 World Trade Center, New York, NY 10048
Silver Futures
Copper Futures
Gold Futures
Zinc Futures
Comex—1978 Report to the Members
Commodity Terminology

New York Mercantile Exchange, 4 World Trade Center, New York, NY 10048
ABC's of Commodities
The New York Mercantile Exchange
Platinum: Metal in Motion
Hedging Energy Futures
A Guide to Imported Lean Beef Futures
Using EFP's in Round White Potato Futures

Minneapolis Grain Exchange, 400 S. Fourth Street, Minneapolis, MN 55415
Hard Amber Durum Wheat
Spring Wheat
Grain Futures Guide
Grain Exchange Overview

New York Cocoa Exchange, 127 John Street, New York, NY 10038
Trading in Cocoa Futures
Understanding the Cocoa Market

New York Coffee & Sugar Exchange, 4 World Trade Center, New York, NY 10048
Trading in Coffee Futures

Trading in Sugar Futures
Significant Changes in the Coffee "C" Contract

New York Cotton Exchange, 4 World Trade Center, New York,
  NY 10048
  Crude Oil Futures
  Cotton Futures
  Futures Trading and Hedging in Frozen Concentrated Orange
    Juice
  Citrus Futures
  Brighter Futures—Liquefied Propane Gas

Amex Commodities Exchange, 86 Trinity Place, New York, NY
  10006
  Rules of the ACE GNMA Futures Contract
  Trading in the ACE GNMA Futures Contract
  Selected Rules of ACE for Associated Persons
  GNMA Yield and Price Equivalent Tables

Kansas City Board of Trade, 4800 Main Street, Suite 274, Kan-
  sas City, MO 64112
  Opportunities in Wheat Futures Trading
  Investment Opportunities
  Membership Directory
  Understanding the Commodity Futures Markets
  Statistical Report
  The Kansas City Board of Trade

CONVERSION FACTORS

Weight	Equivalent
1 Kilogram	2.204622 pounds
1 Metric Quintal	220.14622 pounds
1 Short Ton	2000 pounds
1 Metric Ton	2204.622 pounds
1 Long Ton	2240 pounds
1 Short Ton	.907185 metric tons
1 Long Ton	1.016047 metric tons
1 Short Ton	.892857 Long Tons

60-pound bushels (used for wheat, white potatoes, soybeans)

1 Short Ton	33.333 bushels
1 Metric Ton	36.7437 bushels
1 Long Ton	37.333 bushels

56-pound bushels (used for corn, rye, sorghum grain, flaxseed)
1 Short Ton   35.714 bushels
1 Metric Ton   39.638 bushels
1 Long Ton   40.0 bushels

48-pound bushels (used for barley, buckwheat)
1 Short Ton   41.667 bushels
1 Metric Ton   45.9296 bushels
1 Long Ton   46.667 bushels

38-pound bushels (used for oats)
1 Short Ton   52.63 bushels
1 Metric Ton   58.016 bushels
1 Long Ton   58.94 bushels

THE REGULATOR: COMMODITY FUTURES TRADING COMMISSION

Commodity Futures Trading Commission
2033 K Street, N.W.
Washington, DC 20581
(202) 254-8630

Commissioners:
James Stone, Chairman
Read Dunn
Robert Martin
David Gartner
Gary Seevers (resigned as of June 1)
Donald L. Tendick, Executive Director (202) 254-7556
John Gaine, Office of General Counsel (202) 254-9880
John Field, Director, Enforcement Division (202) 254-7424
Hugh Cadden, Director, Division of Trading and Markets (202) 254-6488
Vernon W. Pherson, Director, Division of Economics and Education (202) 254-3201
Jane Stuckey, Office of Secretariat (202) 254-6314
Bill Monahan, Director, Office of Public Information (202) 254-8630

Regional offices:
Central region headquarters
    233 S. Wacker Drive, Suite 4600
    Chicago, IL 60606
    (312) 353-6642
    Robert Clark, Regional Director

Central region sub-office
 510 Grain Exchange Building
 Minneapolis, MN 55415
 (612) 725-2025
 Joseph Stenger, Division of Trading and Markets

Eastern region headquarters
 1 World Trade Center, Suite 4747
 New York, NY 10048
 (212) 662-0784
 Michael P. Charles, Regional Director

Southwest region headquarters
 4901 Main Street, Room 208
 Kansas City, MO 64112
 (816) 758-2994
 Richard Kirchhoff, Regional Director

Western region headquarters
 2 Embarcadero Center, Suite 1660
 San Francisco, CA 94111
 (415) 556-7503
 Frank N. Masino, Regional Counsel

Hotline numbers:
48 states
 (800) 424-9838
Alaska, Hawaii
 (800) 424-9707
Washington, DC
 (800) 254-7837

TRADING HOURS

Commodity Exchanges	Eastern Daylight	Local Time
Amex Commodities Exchange		
—GNMA Mortgages	9:10– 3:45	
Chicago Board of Trade		
—Iced Broilers	10:15– 2:20	9:15– 1:20
—Silver	9:40– 2:25	8:40– 1:25
—Plywood	10:00– 2:00	9:00– 1:00
—Soybean Meal	10:30– 2:15	9:30– 1:15
—Crude Soybean Oil	10:30– 2:15	9:30– 1:15
—Gold	9:25– 2:35	8:25– 1:35

—GNMA	9:30– 3:45	8:30– 2:45
—GNMA	9:20– 3:45	8:20– 2:45
—Treasury Bonds	9:30– 3:45	8:30– 2:45
—Commercial Paper	9:30– 2:35	8:30– 1:35
—All other contracts	10:30– 2:15	9:30– 1:15

Chicago Mercantile Exchange

—All Cattle Contracts	10:05– 1:45	9:05–12:45
—Eggs	10:20– 2:00	9:20– 1:00
—Russet Burbank Potatoes	10:00– 2:00	9:00– 1:00
—Pork Bellies	10:10– 2:00	9:10– 1:00
—Live Hogs	10:15– 1:55	9:15–12:55
—Hams & Stud Lumber	10:10– 2:00	9:10– 1:00
—Lumber	10:00– 2:05	9:00– 1:05
—Boneless Beef	10:05– 1:45	9:05–12:45
—Milo	10:30– 2:15	9:30– 1:15
—Turkeys	10:10– 1:45	9:10–12:45
—Butter	10:25– 1:35	9:25–12:35
—U.S. Silver Coins	9:50– 2:25	8:50– 1:25
—Gold	9:25– 2:30	8:25– 1:30
—Copper	9:45– 2:15	8:45– 1:15
—T-bills	9:35– 2:35	8:35– 1:35
—T-bills (1-year)	9:20– 2:25	8:20– 1:25
—Canadian Dollars	9:15– 2:22	8:15– 1:22
—Mexican Pesos	9:15– 2:18	8:15– 1:18
—Deutschemarks	9:15– 2:20	8:15– 1:20
—Swiss Francs	9:15– 2:16	8:15– 1:16
—British Pounds	9:15– 2:24	8:15– 1:24
—Japanese Yen	9:15– 2:26	8:15– 1:26
—French Francs	9:15– 2:28	8:15– 1:28
—Dutch Guilders	9:15– 2:30	8:15– 1:30

MidAmerica Commodity Exchange

—Grains	10:30– 2:30	9:30– 1:30
—Silver	9:40– 2:40	8:40– 1:40
—U.S. Silver Coins	9:50– 2:35	8:50– 1:35
—Gold	9:25– 2:40	8:25– 1:40
—Hogs	10:15– 2:05	9:15– 1:05
—Cattle	10:05– 2:00	9:05– 1:00

Commodity Exchange, Inc.

—Gold	9:25– 2:30
—Copper	9:50– 2:00
—Silver	9:40– 2:15
—Zinc	10:15–12:45

Kansas City Board of Trade

—Wheat	10:30– 2:15	9:30– 1:15
—Grain Sorghums	10:30– 2:15	9:30– 1:15

Minneapolis Grain Exchange
—Grains   10:30– 2:15   9:30– 1:15
—Pork Bellies   10:30– 2:00   9:30– 1:00

New York Cocoa Exchange
—Cocoa   9:30– 2:30
—Rubber   9:45– 2:45

New York Coffee & Sugar
—Coffee B   9:45– 2:28°
—Coffee C   9:45– 2:28°
—Sugar #11   10:00– 2:43°°
—Sugar #12   10:00– 2:43°°

    ° 2:30 Closing Call Commences.
    °° 2:45 Closing Call Commences.

New York Cotton Exchange
—Cotton #1   10:30– 2.50
—Cotton #2   10:30– 3:00
—Frozen Concentrated
   Orange Juice   10:15– 2:45
—Propane   9:45– 2:35
—Crude Oil   9:50– 2:20

New York Mercantile Exchange
—Round White Potatoes   9:50– 2:00
—Platinum   9:30– 2:30
—Palladium   9:50– 2:20
—Gold (Kilo & 400 oz)   9:25– 2:30
—U.S. Silver Coins   9:35– 2:15
—Imported Lean Beef   10:15– 1:45
—No. 2 Heating Oil   10:30– 2:18
—No. 6 Industrial Fuel Oil 10:35– 2:20
—Swiss Francs   9:00– 2:44
—Deutschemarks   9:02– 2:48
—Canadian Dollars   9:04– 2:52
—British Pounds   9:06– 2:56
—Japanese Yen   9:08– 3:00

OTHER BOOKS ON FUTURES

The Case Against Floating Exchanges. Einzig, Paul, St. Martin's
   Press
Charting Commodity Market Price Behavior. Belveal, L. Dee,
   Commodities Press

Commodities: A Chart Anthology. Dobson, Edward D., Traders Press

Commodities: Now Through 1984. Bernstein, Jake, MBH Commodity Advisors

Commodity Futures as a Business Management Tool. Arthur, Henry B., Harvard University Press

Commodity Futures for Profit . . . A Farmer's Guide to Hedging. Oster, Merrill J., Investor Publications Inc.

The Commodity Futures Game—Who Wins? Who Loses? Why? Teweles, Harlow, and Stone, McGraw-Hill

The Commodity Futures Market Guide. Kroll, Stanley, and Shishko, Irwin, Harper & Row Publishers, Inc.

Commodity Futures Trading. A Bibliographic Guide. Woy, James B., R. R. Bowker Co.

Commodity Futures Trading: Bibliography Cumulative through 1976. Chicago Board of Trade

The Commodity Futures Trading Guide. Teweles, Stone, and Harlow. McGraw-Hill

Commodity Futures Trading with Moving Averages. Maxwell, J. R., Speer Books

Commodity Futures Trading Orders. Maxwell, J. R., Speer Books

Commodity Futures Trading with Point-and-Figure Charts. Maxwell, Joseph R., Sr., Speer Books

Commodity Futures Trading with Stops. Maxwell, J. R., Speer Books

Commodity Speculation with Profits in Mind. Belveal, L. Dee. Commodities Press

Commodity Spreads: A Historical Chart Perspective. Dobson, Edward D., Traders Press

Commodity Trading Manual. Chicago Board of Trade

Commodity Trading Manual. Gould, Bruce, Bruce Gould Publications

Commodity Trading Systems and Methods. Kaufman, P. J., Wiley-Interscience

Commodity Yearbook. Commodity Research Bureau, Inc.

Commodity Yearbook Statistical Abstract Service. Commodity Research Bureau

The Dow Jones Commodities Handbook. Ruck, Dan, editor, Dow Jones Books

Dow Jones–Irwin Guide to Commodities Trading. Gould, Bruce, Dow Jones–Irwin

Economics of Futures Trading (2nd edition). Hieronymus, Thomas A., Commodity Research Bureau, Inc.

The Elliott Wave Principle. Bolton, A. H., Monetary Research Ltd.

Elliott Wave Principle. Prechter, Robert R., Jr., and Frost, A. J., New Classics Library

The Fastest Game in Town. Reinach, Anthony, Commodity Research Bureau, Inc.

Getting Started in Commodity Futures Trading. Powers, Mark J., Investor Publications

How to Make Money in Commodities. Gould, Bruce, Bruce Gould Publications

How to Use the Money Market Futures Contracts. Schwarz, Edward, Dow Jones–Irwin

Modern Commodity Futures Trading. Gold, Gerald, Commodity Research Bureau, Inc.

The Momentum-Gap Method. Miller, Lowell, G. P. Putnam's Sons

Multiply Your Money . . . A Beginner's Guide to Commodity Speculation. Oster, Merrill J., Investor Publications Inc.

Point and Figure Commodity Trading Techniques. Zieg, Kermit C., Kaufman, Perry J., Investors Intelligence

The Power of Leverage. Jenkins, David, Investors Intelligence

The Professional Commodity Trader. Kroll, Stanley, Harper & Row Publishers, Inc.

A Professional Guide to Commodity Speculation. Shaw, John E., Prentice-Hall

Scientific Interpretation of Bar Charts. Hill, J. R., Commodity Research Institute

Sensible Speculating in Commodities. Angrist, Stanley W., Simon and Schuster

Success in Commodities . . . the Congestion Phase System. Nofri, Eugene, and Steinberg, Jeanette, Success in Commodities

A Timing Method for Fundamentalists. Gehm, F., F. Gehm and Associates

The Wave Principle. Elliott, R. N., Monetary Research Ltd.

What Makes You a Winner or Loser in the Stock and Commodity Markets? Hayden, Jack, Investors Intelligence

Winning in the Commodities Market. Angell, George, Doubleday and Co., Inc.

VII. The Futures Market: The Lingo of the Game

A special thanks goes to the Chicago Board of Trade, which provided much of the material on which the following definitions are based.

ACCOUNT EXECUTIVE—see BROKER; FLOOR BROKER; REGISTERED COMMODITY REPRESENTATIVE.

ACCUMULATE—increasing one's commodity position with purchases over a period of time, and at differing prices, rather than acquiring the large position all in one transaction and at one price.

ACREAGE ALLOTMENT—a program established by the federal government that is aimed at boosting production of crops that are scarce and diminishing production of crops that are plentiful.

ACTUALS—the physical or cash commodity on which the futures contracts are based. See also CASH COMMODITY; PHYSICAL COMMODITY.

AFLOAT—physical commodities still in transit.

ARBITRAGE—an investing technique where the customer simultaneously buys and sells contracts on two commodities in the expectation that the discrepancy in prices between the two will result in profit.

ARBITRATION—submitting a dispute to a third party, usually agreed to beforehand, who will hear arguments from both sides and then reach a decision.

AT THE MARKET—an order to purchase or sell a contract at the best possible price prevailing in the market.

BACKWARDATION—expression used in New York markets meaning nearby contracts are trading at premium to deferred months.

BASIS—the difference in price between the futures contract and the underlying physical commodity.

BASIS GRADE—a specific grade named in an exchange's futures contract. Other grades than that specificed are subject to price alterations.

BEAR—a trader who believes that prices will decline.

BEAR MARKET—a market where prices are declining.

BID—an offer made on the floor of an exchange to buy a specific quantity of futures contracts at a specific price.

BOARD OF TRADE—in a general sense, any exchange where commodities are bought and sold.

BREAK—a fast, but sharp, decline in prices.

BROAD TAPE—in a general sense, a newswire that carries prices and stories about the securities and futures markets.

BROKER—a person paid a fee or commission for transacting buy or sell orders. See also FLOOR BROKER; REGISTERED COMMODITY REPRESENTATIVE.

BROKERAGE—the fee a broker charges for his services. It may be a flat charge or based on a percentage. See also COMMISSION.

BROKERAGE HOUSE—the firm which handles buy and sell orders, on a commission basis, for customers.

BUCKET, BUCKETING—the illegal practice of accepting orders from a client without executing them, or the illegal practice of using a customer's principal—margin deposit—without disclosing such use.

BULGE—a rapid, but temporary, increase in prices.

BULL—a trader who believes that prices will rise.

BULL MARKET—a market where prices are rising.

BULLION—silver or gold in bars or ingots of a specified quality.

BUYER'S CALL—see CALL.

BUY IN—making purchases in the market to cover a previous sale. See also COVER; EVENING UP; SHORT COVER.

BUY ON CLOSE—to buy contracts near the end of a day's trading at a price near the closing price.

BUY ON OPENING—to buy contracts near the start of a day's trading at a price near the opening price.

BUYING HEDGE—purchasing contracts to protect against the possibility of increased costs of commodities that might be needed in the future. See also HEDGING.

C&F—cost and freight paid to port of destination.

CFTC—the Commodity Futures Trading Commission, which regulates the futures markets.

C.I.F.—cost, insurance, and freight paid to port of destination.

CALL—the period in which the price for each futures contract is established—for example, the opening or closing call. A BUYER'S CALL is the purchase of a specified quantity and grade of a commodity at a certain number of points above or below a specific delivery month in futures, with the buyer being allowed a certain period of time within which to fix the price by either purchasing a futures contract for the account of the seller or indicating to the seller when he wishes to fix the price. A SELLER'S CALL is similar to the buyer's call except that the seller has the right to determine the time to fix the price.

CARRYING CHARGES—costs incurred in warehousing the actual commodity, usually including storage, insurance, and interest charges. A FULL CARRYING CHARGE MARKET is when the price differences in the futures market between delivery months reflect the full carrying charges.

CARRY-OVER—current supplies of the actual commodity which are from previous production or marketing seasons.

CASH COMMODITY—the actual commodity on which the futures contract is based. See also ACTUALS; PHYSICAL COMMODITY.

CASH MARKET—the market in which transactions for the purchase and sale of the actual physical commodity are made. It can refer to an organized central market, such as the cash section of a futures exchange, or the stockyards in the livestock industry. See also SPOT.

CERTIFICATED STOCK—stock of the actual physical commodity which has been inspected and deemed to be of a quality deliverable against the futures contracts. These stocks are stored at the delivery points approved by the exchange.

CHARTING—using graphs and charts in technical analysis to track trends of price movement, and volume and open interest. See also TECHNICAL ANALYSIS.

CHURNING—practice whereby a broker will make numerous buy and sell transactions in a customer's account to generate more commission.

CLEARINGHOUSE—an agency affiliated with a futures exchange through which contracts are settled, guaranteed, and later either offset or fulfilled through delivery of the commodity, and through which financial settlement is made.

CLEARING PRICE—see SETTLEMENT PRICE.

CLOSING RANGE—a range of closely related prices at which transactions take place at the closing of the market.

COMMISSION—see BROKERAGE.

COMMISSION MERCHANT—a person who makes a trade either for another member of the exchange or for a nonmember client, but who makes the trade in his own name and becomes liable as principal to the other party in the transaction.

COMMODITY CREDIT CORPORATION (CCC)—a government-owned corporation established in 1933 to assist U.S. agriculture. Its major operations are price-support programs in which it purchases excess supplies of crops and provides assistance in foreign exports.

COMMODITY FUTURES TRADING COMMISSION—a federal regulatory agency charged under the Commodity Futures Trading

Commission Act of 1974 with regulating the futures markets. It replaced the Commodity Exchange Authority, which was an arm of the Department of Agriculture.

CONTRACT GRADES—standards for commodities that are listed in the rules of the exchanges. The grades must be met when delivering the actual commodity against futures contracts. See also DELIVERABLE GRADES; SAMPLE GRADE.

CONTROLLED ACCOUNT—see DISCRETIONARY ACCOUNT.

CORNER—to buy or sell a position in the futures market that is so large that the trader controls the market and can manipulate prices.

COVER—to offset a previous futures transaction with an equally sized opposite transaction. A SHORT COVER is the purchase of futures contracts to cover an earlier sale of an equal number of the same delivery month. See also BUY IN; EVENING UP.

CRUSH—process for reducing soybeans to meal and oil.

CURRENT DELIVERY MONTH—the futures contract that will come due, and become deliverable, during the current calendar month.

DAY ORDER—a buy or sell order that automatically is cancelled if it is not filled during the day entered.

DAY TRADER—a speculator who liquidates his futures positions prior to the close of the same trading session.

DEFAULT—a decision by a producer of commodities not to repay a government loan, but instead to surrender his crops; or, in the futures markets, the theoretical failure of a party to a futures contract to either make or take delivery of the physical commodity as required under the contract.

DEFERRED DELIVERY—the more distant months in which futures trading is taking place, as distinguished from the nearby futures delivery months.

DELIVERABLE GRADES—see CONTRACT GRADES; SAMPLE GRADE.

DELIVERY—basically, the changing of ownership or control of a commodity under very specific terms and procedures established by the exchange upon which the contract is traded.

DELIVERY NOTICE—see NOTICE OF INTENTION TO DELIVER.

DELIVERY POINTS—those locations and facilities designated by a commodity exchange at which stocks of a commodity may be delivered in fulfillment of a contract, under procedures established by the exchange.

DEMAND ELASTICITY—see ELASTICITY.

DIFFERENTIALS—price differences between classes, grades, and locations of different stocks of the same commodity.

DISCOUNT—a downward adjustment in price allowed for delivery of stocks of a commodity of lesser-than-contract grade against a futures contract; or, the price differences between futures of different delivery months.

DISCRETIONARY ACCOUNT—an arrangement by which the holder of the account gives written power of attorney to another, often his broker, to make buying and selling decisions without notification to the holder.

ECONOMETRICS—the application of statistical and mathematical methods in the field of economics in testing and quantifying economic theories and the solution of economic problems.

ELASTICITY—a characteristic of commodities that describes the interaction of the supply, demand, and price of a commodity. A commodity is said to be reflecting DEMAND ELASTICITY when a price change creates an increase or decrease in consumption. SUPPLY ELASTICITY is what occurs when a change in price creates a change in the production of the commodity. INELASTICITY occurs when either supply or demand fails to respond to the price changes.

EVENING UP—see BUY IN; COVER.

F.O.B.—free on board; indicates that all delivery, inspection, and loading costs involved in putting a commodity on board a carrier have been paid.

FEED RATIOS—the variable relationship of the cost of feeding the animals to their market weight to their sales prices, expressed as ratios.

FILL OR KILL (FOK) ORDER—an order in the futures markets that must be filled immediately, at the price specified, or it automatically is cancelled.

FIRST NOTICE DAY—the first day on which notices of intent to deliver the commodity in fulfillment of a given month's futures contract can be made by the seller to the clearinghouse and by the clearinghouse to a buyer.

FLOOR BROKER—see BROKER; REGISTERED COMMODITY REPRESENTATIVE.

FORWARD CONTRACT—a transaction in the cash market in which two parties agree to the purchase and sale of a commodity at some future time under such conditions as the two agree. In contrast to a FUTURES CONTRACT, a forward contract's terms are not standardized; a forward contract is not transferable and usually can be cancelled only with the consent of the other party, which often must be obtained for consideration and under penalty; and forward contracts are not traded in federally designated contract markets. Essentially, a forward contract is any cash market transaction for which delivery is not made "on the spot." See also FUTURES CONTRACT.

FREE SUPPLY—stocks of a commodity which are available for commercial sale, as opposed to those that are government owned or controlled.

FULL CARRYING CHARGE—see CARRYING CHARGES.

FUNDAMENTAL ANALYSIS—an analytical approach to market behavior that stresses the underlying factors of supply and demand in the commodity, in the belief that such analysis can predict future price trends.

FUTURES CONTRACT—an agreement to make or take delivery of a standardized amount of a commodity, of standardized minimum quality grades, during a specific month, under terms and conditions established by a federally designated contract market upon which trading is conducted, at a price established in the trading pit.

GRAIN FUTURES ACT—a federal statute that regulates trading in grain futures.

GROSS PROCESSING MARGIN (GPM)—the difference between the cost of soybeans and the combined sales income of the soybean oil and meal that results from processing soybeans. Other industries have similar formulas to express the relationship of raw-material costs to sales income from finished products.

HEDGING—taking a position in a futures market that is intended as a temporary substitute for the sale or purchase of the actual commodity; the sale of futures contracts in anticipation of future sales of cash commodities as a protection against possible price declines, or the purchase of futures contracts in anticipation of future purchases of cash commodities as a protection against the possibility of increasing costs.

INELASTICITY—see ELASTICITY.

INITIAL MARGIN—the initial funds required by a brokerage house to establish a position in the futures market.

INVERTED MARKET—futures market in which the nearer months are selling at premiums to the more distant months; characteristically, a market in which supplies are currently in shortage.

INVISIBLE SUPPLY—uncounted stocks of a commodity in the hands of wholesalers, manufacturers, and producers, which cannot be identified accurately; stocks outside commercial channels but theoretically available to the market.

JOB LOT—a quantity of a commodity larger or smaller in size than the corresponding futures contract for that commodity. See ROUND LOT.

LAST TRADING DAY—the day on which trading ceases for the maturing delivery month.

LEVERAGE—the power a futures market trader accrues by only risking a small amount of money to obtain a large market position.

LIFE OF CONTRACT—the period between the beginning of trading in a particular future and the expiration of trading in the delivery month.

LIMIT MOVE—the maximum increase or decrease a price may change from the previous session's close.

LIMIT ONLY—the definite price stated by a customer to a

broker restricting the execution of an order to buy for not more than or to sell for not less than the stated price.

LIMIT ORDER—an order in which the customer sets a limit on either price or time of execution, or both, as contrasted with a MARKET ORDER, which implies that the order should be filled at the most favorable price as soon as possible. See also MARKET ORDER.

LIMITS—see also POSITION LIMIT; PRICE LIMITS; VARIABLE LIMITS.

LIQUIDATION—taking a position in the futures market that closes out a previous position. For example, selling contracts that previously were purchased. See BUY IN; COVER; EVENING UP.

LIQUID MARKET—a market where selling and buying can be accomplished with ease, due to the presence of a large number of interested buyers and sellers willing and able to trade substantial quantities at small price differences.

LOAN PROGRAM—primary means of government agricultural price-support operations, in which the government lends money to farmers at preannounced rates with the farmers' crops used as collateral. Default on these loans is the primary method by which the government acquires stocks of agricultural commodities.

LONG—as a noun, one who has bought futures contracts or the cash commodity (depending upon the market under discussion) and has not yet offset that position. As a verb (going long), the action of taking a position in which one has bought futures contracts (or the cash commodity) without taking the offsetting action.

MANAGED ACCOUNT—see DISCRETIONARY ACCOUNT.

MARGIN—money deposited by both buyers and sellers of futures contracts to insure performance of the terms of the contract (the delivery or taking of delivery of the commodity or the cancellation of the position by a subsequent offsetting trade). Margin in commodities is not a payment of equity or down payment on the commodity itself but rather is a performance bond or security deposit. See also INITIAL MARGIN.

MARGIN CALL—a call from a clearinghouse to a clearing member, or from a brokerage firm to a customer, to bring margin deposits up to a required minimum level.

MARKET ORDER—an order to buy or sell futures contracts that is to be filled at the best possible price and as soon as possible. In contrast to a LIMIT ORDER, which may specify requirements for price or time of execution. See also LIMIT ORDER.

MATURITY—a period within which a futures contract can be settled by delivery of the actual commodity; the period between the first notice day and the last trading day of a commodity futures contract.

MEMBER'S RATE—commission charged for the execution of an order for a person who is a member of the exchange.

MOVING AVERAGE—a system used by technical analysts for averaging near-term prices relative to long-term prices.

NEARBY DELIVERY MONTH—the futures contract closest to maturity.

NOMINAL PRICE—declared price for a futures month sometimes used in place of a closing price when no recent trading has taken place in that particular delivery month; usually an average of the bid and asked prices.

NOTICE DAY—see FIRST NOTICE DAY.

NOTICE OF INTENTION TO DELIVER—a notice that must be presented by the seller to the clearinghouse. The clearinghouse then assigns the notice, and the subsequent delivery instrument to the longest-standing buyer on record. Under Chicago Board of Trade rules, for example, such notices must be presented by 8:00 p.m. of the second business day prior to the day on which delivery is to be made.

OFFER—an indication of willingness to sell at a given price; the opposite of BID. See also BID.

OFFSET—the liquidation of a purchase of futures through the sale of an equal number of contracts of the same delivery month, or the covering of a short sale of futures contracts through the purchase of an equal number of contracts of the same delivery month. Either action transfers the obligation to make or take delivery of the actual commodity to another principal.

OMNIBUS ACCOUNT—an account carried by one futures commission merchant with another in which the transactions of two or more persons are combined rather than designated separately and the identity of the individual accounts is not disclosed.

ON TRACK (OR TRACK COUNTRY STATION)—a type of deferred delivery in which the price is set F.O.B. seller's location and the buyer agrees to pay freight costs to his destination. See also F.O.B.

ONE CANCELS THE OTHER (OCO) ORDER—an order in the futures market where a trader enters orders on both sides of the trading range with the stipulation that when one is filled the other is cancelled.

OPENING RANGE—range of closely related prices at which transactions take place at the opening of the market; buying and selling orders at the opening might be filled at any point within such a range.

OPEN INTEREST—the total number of futures contracts of a given commodity that have not yet been offset by opposite futures transactions nor fulfilled by delivery of the commodity; the total number of open transactions. Each open transaction has a buyer and a seller, but for calculation of open interest, only one side of the contract is counted.

OPEN ORDER—an order in the futures market which stays open to be filled until the specified price is reached or the order cancelled.

OPEN OUTCRY—a method of public auction for making verbal bids and offers in the trading pits or rings of commodity exchanges.

ORIGINAL MARGIN—see INITIAL MARGIN.

OVERBOUGHT—a technical opinion that the market price has risen too steeply and too fast in relation to underlying fundamental factors.

OVERSOLD—a technical opinion that the market price has declined too steeply and too fast in relation to underlying fundamental factors.

P&S (PURCHASE AND SALE) STATEMENT—a statement sent by a commission house to a customer when his futures position has changed, showing the number of contracts involved, the prices at which the contracts were bought or sold, the gross profit or loss, the commission charges, and the net profit or loss on the transactions.

PARITY—a theoretically equal relationship between farm product prices and all other prices. In farm program legislation, parity is defined in such a manner that the purchasing power of a unit of an agricultural commodity is maintained at its level during an earlier historical base period.

PHYSICAL COMMODITY—see ACTUALS; CASH COMMODITY.

PIT—the ring on the exchange trading floor where trading takes place.

POSITION—a market commitment. A buyer of futures contracts is said to have a long position and, conversely, a seller of futures contracts is said to have a short position.

POSITION LIMIT—the maximum number of speculative futures contracts one can hold as determined by the Commodity Futures Trading Commission and/or the exchange upon which the contract is traded. See also PRICE LIMITS; TRADING LIMIT; VARIABLE LIMITS.

POSITION TRADING—an approach to trading in which the trader either buys or sells contracts and holds them for an extended period of time, as distinguished from the DAY TRADER, who will normally initiate and offset his position within a single trading session. See also DAY TRADER.

PREMIUM—the additional payment allowed by exchange regulations for delivery of higher-than-required standards or grades of a commodity against a futures contract. In speaking of price relationships between different delivery months of a given commodity, one is said to be "trading at a premium" over another when its price is greater than that of the other.

PRICE LIMITS—the maximum price advance or decline from

the previous day's settlement price permitted for a contract in one trading session by the rules of the exchange. See also VARI-ABLE LIMITS; POSITION LIMIT.

PRIVATE WIRES—wires leased by various firms and news agencies for the transmission of information to branch offices and subscriber clients.

PUBLIC ELEVATORS—grain-storage facilities, licensed and regulated by state and federal agencies, in which space is rented out to whoever is willing to pay for it; some are also approved by the commodity exchanges as regular for delivery of commodities against futures contracts.

PYRAMIDING—the use of profits on existing futures positions as margins to increase the size of the position, normally in successively smaller increments; such as the use of profits on the purchase of five futures contracts as margin to purchase an additional four contracts, whose profits will in turn be used to margin an additional three contracts, etc.

RANGE—the difference between the highest and lowest prices recorded during a given trading session, week, month, year, etc.

REGISTERED COMMODITY REPRESENTATIVE (RCR)—see BROKER; FLOOR BROKER.

REGULARITY—term used to describe a processing plant, warehouse, mill, vault, or bank that satisfies exchange requirements in terms of financing, facilities, capacity, and location, and has been approved as acceptable for delivery of commodities against futures contracts.

REGULATED COMMODITIES—effective April 1975, U.S. futures markets in all commodities became regulated under the Commodity Exchange Act as amended by the Commodity Futures Trading Act of 1974. Trading by U.S. citizens on foreign futures markets, such as London silver, is not regulated.

REPORTING LIMIT, REPORTABLE POSITION—the number of futures contracts, as determined by the Commodity Futures Trading Commission, above which one must report daily to the exchange and the CFTC with regard to the size of one's position by commodity, by delivery month, and by purpose of the trading.

RETENDER—the right of holders of futures contracts who have been tendered a delivery notice through the clearinghouse to offer the notice for sale on the open market, liquidating their obligation to take delivery under the contract; applicable only to certain commodities and only within a specified period of time.

RING—see PIT.

ROUND LOT—a quantity of a commodity equal in size to the corresponding futures contract for the commodity, as distinguished from a JOB LOT, which may be larger or smaller than the contract. See also JOB LOT.

ROUND TURN—the combination of an initiating purchase or sale of a futures contract and the offsetting sale or purchase of an equal number of futures contracts of the same delivery month. Commission fees for commodities transactions cover the round turn.

SAMPLE GRADE—in commodities, usually the lowest quality acceptable for delivery in satisfaction of futures contracts. See also CONTRACT GRADES.

SCALPER—a futures trader who attempts to make profits by entering and exiting the market in short periods of time.

SELLER'S CALL—see CALL.

SELLING HEDGE (OR SHORT HEDGE)—selling futures contracts to protect against possible decreased prices of commodities which will be sold in the future. See also HEDGING.

SETTLEMENT PRICE—the price established by a clearinghouse at the close of each trading session as the official price to be used in determining net gains or losses, margin requirements, and the next day's price limits. The term "settlement price" is also often used as an approximate equivalent to the term "closing price." The close in futures trading refers to a very brief period of time at the end of the trading day, during which transactions frequently take place quickly and at a range of prices immediately before the bell. Therefore, there frequently is no one "closing price" but a range of closing prices. The settlement price is the closing price if there is only one closing price. When there is a closing range, it is as near to the midpoint of the closing range as possible, consistent with the contract's increments. Thus, the settlement price can be used to provide a single reference point for analysis of closing market conditions.

SHORT—as a noun, one who has sold futures contracts or the cash commodity (depending upon the market under discussion) and has not yet offset that position. As a verb, the action of taking a position in which one has sold futures contracts (or made a forward contract for sale of the cash commodity) without taking the offsetting action.

SHORT COVER—see COVER.

SPECULATOR—in an economic sense, one who attempts to anticipate commodity price changes and to profit through the sale and purchase or purchase and sale of commodity futures contracts or of the physical commodity.

SPOT—refers to the characteristic of being available for immediate (or nearly immediate) delivery. An outgrowth of the phrase "on the spot," it usually refers to a cash market price for stocks of the physical commodity that are available for immediate delivery. Spot is also sometimes used in reference to the futures contract of the current month, in which case trading is still "futures" trading but delivery is possible at any time. See also CASH MARKET.

SPOT MONTH—see CURRENT DELIVERY MONTH.

SPREADING—the purchase of one futures contract and sale of another, in the expectation that the price relationships between the two will change so that a subsequent offsetting sale and purchase will yield a net profit. Examples include the purchase of one delivery month and the sale of another in the same commodity on the same exchange, or the purchase and sale of the same delivery month in the same commodity on different exchanges, or the purchase of one commodity and the sale of another (wheat vs. corn or corn vs. hogs), or the purchase of one commodity and the sale of the products of that commodity (soybeans vs. soybean oil and soybean meal).

STOP ORDER—an order in the futures market which instructs that a trader's position be liquidated when a certain price is hit. Used to protect profits or guard against losses.

SUPPLY ELASTICITY—see ELASTICITY.

SWITCH—liquidation of a position in one delivery month of a commodity and simultaneous initiation of a similar position in another delivery month of the same commodity. When used by hedgers, this tactic is referred to as rolling forward the hedge.

TECHNICAL ANALYSIS—an approach to analysis of futures markets and future trends of commodity prices that examines the technical factors of market activity. Technical analysts normally examine patterns of price change, rates of change, and changes in volume of trading and open interest, often by charting, in the hope of being able to predict and profit from future trends. Compare with FUNDAMENTAL ANALYSIS.

TENDER—the act on the part of the seller of futures contracts of giving notice to the clearinghouse that he intends to deliver the physical commodity in satisfaction of the futures contract. The clearinghouse in turn passes along the notice to oldest buyer of record in that delivery month of the commodity. See also RETENDER.

TICKER TAPE—a continuous paper-tape transmission of commodity or security prices, volume, and other trading and market information, which operates on private leased wires by the exchanges, available to their member firms and other interested parties on a subscription basis.

TO-ARRIVE CONTRACT—a type of deferred shipment in which the price is based on delivery at the destination point and the seller pays the freight in shipping it to that point.

TRADING LIMIT—standards adopted by a futures exchange relating to the number of contracts that may be held or to the price change that a contract can undergo in any one day.

VARIABLE LIMITS—a Chicago Board of Trade price limit system that allows for larger than normally allowable price movements under certain circumstances, as follows:

If three or more contracts within a crop year (or all contracts in a crop year if there are less than three open contracts) close on the limit bid (lower) for three successive business days or on the limit sellers (higher) for three successive business days, then the limit would become 150 percent of the current level for all contract months and remain there for three successive business days.

If three or more contract months (or all contracts in a crop year if there are less than three open contracts) in a given crop year close on the limit bid for the next three business days or on the limit sellers for three successive business days, then the limits will remain at 150 percent of the original level for another three-day period.

The limits would remain at 150 percent for successive periods of three business days until three or more contracts in a crop year (or all contracts in a crop year if there are less than three open contracts) do not close at the limit on one day during that period. If, at any time during a three-day business period, the three or more contract months (or all contracts in a crop year if there are less than three open contracts) do not close on the limit bid or limit sellers then the limits would revert to their original level at the end of the three-day period. See also PRICE LIMITS; POSITION LIMIT.

VARIATION MARGIN CALL—a call for additional margin deposits made by a clearinghouse to a clearing member while trading is in progress when current price trends have substantially reduced the clearing member's margin deposits. Variation calls are payable within the hour.

VENTURE CAPITAL—monies not needed for routine living expenses and basic savings that are available for purposes of investing or speculating.

WAREHOUSE RECEIPT—document guaranteeing the existence and availability of a given quantity and quality of a commodity in storage; commonly used as the instrument of transfer of ownership in both cash and futures transactions.

WASH SALES—illegal and fictitious transactions where persons simultaneously buy and sell futures to indicate an actual market. Used to manipulate prices for tax purposes.

Index

208　　　　　　　　　　　　　　　　　　　　　　　　　INDEX